The Relationship
Doctor's
Prescription
FOR X

Healing
a Hurting
Relationship

Dr. David Hawkins

HARVEST HOUSE PUBLISHERS

EUGENE, OREGON

THE RELATIONSHIP DOCTOR'S PRESCRIPTION FOR HEALING A HURTING RELATIONSHIP
Copyright © 2006 by David Hawkins
Published by Harvest House Publishers
Eugene, Oregon 97402
www.harvesthousepublishers.com

Library of Congress Cataloging-in-Publication Data
Hawkins, David, 1951–
The relationship doctor's prescription for healing a hurting relationship / David Hawkins.
    p. cm.
Includes bibliographical references.
ISBN-13: 978-0-7369-1838-1 (pbk.)
ISBN-10: 0-7369-1838-8 (pbk.)
1. Man-woman relationships—Religious aspects—Christianity. 2. Marriage—Religious aspects—Christianity. I. Title.
BV4596.M3H395 2006
248.8'44—dc22   2006002479

Printed in the United States of America

06 07 08 09 10 11 12 13 14 / BP-CF / 10 9 8 7 6 5 4 3 2 1

Contents

A Note from the Author

A marriage that appears headed for failure. Love that has lost its vitality. A relationship seemingly stuck in a chasm between life and death.

Do you feel as if you're in a relationship or marriage headed for disaster? Nothing can be more excruciating. Everything else in life fades as we feel overwhelmed and question whether our relationship can be restored.

The Relationship Doctor's Prescription for Healing a Hurting Relationship provides practical tools that will help you repair your most important relationship. You will discover that even difficult relationships need not fail. Although they can be extremely challenging, where there is a problem, there is a solution. This book will help you accurately identify your relational problems and offer strategies for repairing your relationship.

Please join me, *The Relationship Doctor,* on a path toward understanding your unique relational problem—and healing it. Together, with God's help, we can re-create a dynamic and fulfilling relationship.

1

The Four Horsemen
of a Relational Apocalypse

"Listen to your body."

This well-worn advice comes from coaches training their premier athletes, doctors assisting their patients—and yes, even psychologists working with their clients. Listen to your body because symptoms, in the form of feelings, can tell us a lot about the origins of our problems and how we can solve them.

Several years ago, I threw this advice out the window. I thought I knew better than my body. At 40, I was training for my first marathon. As a neophyte marathoner, I imagined coasting across the finish line to the roar of well-wishers. With that image in mind, I pushed the limits, didn't listen to my symptoms of pain, sprained my ankle, and was unable to compete on race day. Visions of glory evaporated under the harsh glare of a broken-down body. After spending three months in training and logging over 200 miles in running, I stood hobbled on the sidelines, watching my training partners compete.

The situation was absurd because I brought the calamity on myself by *ignoring my symptoms*. I felt the nagging soreness in my ankle but decided not to heed the warning. I "pushed through it," following ill-advised counsel from some friends. I kept running despite the pain. I refused to pay attention to the swelling in my ankle. I taped it, not only to keep the swelling down but also to hide it from myself. I didn't want to see what was happening. I had one goal in mind—to compete and excel in the Portland Marathon. Ignorance turned to injury and loss.

In retrospect, I see the error of my ways and am embarrassed by my bullheadedness. I wish I had paid attention to my body. I wish I had thought about my symptoms. I wish I had listened to the doctor. Had I done that, I might have run that marathon. I might have rested, slowed my training, and accomplished my goal.

You have picked up this copy of *The Relationship Doctor's Prescription for Healing a Hurting Relationship* because you are looking for answers to some of the most painful problems you will ever confront. You have experienced, or are experiencing, a hurting relationship and know full well the agony it can bring. You know intimately that when our relationships are not going well, we do not do well. Like a swollen ankle, a broken relationship can hobble us and eventually bring us to our knees.

In these pages you will learn how ignoring symptoms in your relationship can bring you needless trouble. And more importantly, you will find practical solutions for these nagging problems.

Join me as we consider why you might be hurting and what you can do to build the kind of relationship you really want.

The Problems Won't Just Go Away

Terri has been counseling with me for more than a year. At 47, she appears tired and much older than she is. She tells me she's gained more than 50 pounds over the past four years. She no longer cares about her appearance, dressing in worn baggy clothes that mirror her demeanor, which is drawn and discouraged. Terri admits to drinking a glass or two of wine every night to deaden her sorrow.

Terri has lost hope for an intimate and loving relationship with her husband, Ken, and she has grown to accept the distance and lack of intimacy.

Terri's husband meets with us when his work allows, but he has made it clear that work comes first. Recently Teri missed an appointment, which is very unusual. When I called to ask her what had happened, she sounded more discouraged than usual.

"I waited for Ken to join us," she said. "He hasn't come home yet, so I decided not to come in." I heard a deep sigh.

"How are things going?" I asked.

"About the same," she said slowly. "We don't really have anything new to share. Ken's been working a lot, and we haven't practiced any of the things we talked about last time. I don't think anything is changing."

"You sound pretty discouraged, Terri."

"I hate feeling like this. I hate it. I don't think Ken wants to change, but I do. I'm not sure I can live like this anymore."

"That's often the way it is," I said. "One person has more motivation to change than the other. Usually, but not always, it's the woman. Men seem to be able to settle in and accept things the way they are. I've noticed that Ken doesn't seem committed to the counseling process."

"I guess I try to forget about our problems," Terri said. "I don't want to face the fact that our marriage is going downhill. I don't like to think about how discouraged and depressed I really am."

"I have three questions for you to consider, Terri. First, how are you really feeling?"

"Well, I'm feeling really down. Ken and I don't have much of a relationship. We haven't gone back to church. We don't do anything fun anymore. Even after talking about it in counseling, we haven't done anything special. He doesn't seem interested in me. He spends all of his time and energy at work. I feel like I'm just wasting away. I spend time with my friends, but it's not the same as having a loving relationship with my husband."

"I'm not happy that you're discouraged," I said carefully. "But your feelings are symptoms, and they're telling us that something is terribly wrong. Your discouragement and depression are friends, at least in the sense that they are warning signs. You need more from Ken, right?"

"Absolutely. But nothing seems to change, no matter how much I want it to."

"I've heard a saying that applies here: 'If you do what you've always done, you'll get what you've always gotten.' Can you see that happening to you?"

"Yes," she said. "I know I settle for distance when I want closeness. I settle for criticism when I want someone who admires and appreciates me. I know I am covering my pain with alcohol. I want Ken to be as committed as I am to having fun together—creating some adventure in our marriage. It's boring and painful, and I don't like it."

"Yes, Terri. I think you are saying what is really true for you. I can see the distance in your marriage and the pain it causes you. I wonder if Ken doesn't work so many hours to avoid the pain in the marriage too. He can't be all that happy with the way things are."

"I think about that. Is he really satisfied with things? I can't believe he is."

"Now, my second question. If things were to stay exactly the same for the next 20 years, how would you feel?"

"Oh, man," she blurted. "I'd hate it! Just thinking about it makes me shiver. I don't want to imagine my life being this way in the future."

"Tell me a little more about that," I said, hoping Terri would feel the immensity of what she seemed ready to express. I wanted her to *embrace her symptoms.* I wanted her to feel how unhappy she was.

I wanted her to really accept her unhappiness and recognize that change was a necessity, not simply something that would be nice.

"I'm not sure I want to think about things being this way for another 20 years," she said.

"I'm not asking you to settle for things the way they are, Terri," I said. "Quite the opposite. I want you to feel what you are feeling. Remember—emotions are *e-motions—energy in motion.* They help us know what we need and give us the energy to move there."

"Okay, I'll say it. I hate the distance I feel between us. I hate that Ken won't come to counseling. I hate that he loves his work more than he loves me. I hate thinking of my marriage being like this for another 20 years. I won't live like this."

I could hear the energy in her voice. I could hear the anger at her situation.

"Are you ready for my third question?" I asked.

"Fire away," she said.

"Considering how you feel right now about Ken and your marriage, are you willing to create a crisis? Are you willing to take some dramatic steps to insist on change?"

I waited for her answer, wondering if she was finally willing to take big steps toward healing their broken relationship. Like Terri and Ken, so many couples I counsel simply settle in and accept things for what they are, not realizing how damaged their relationship is until too late.

As I waited for Terri's answer, I said a silent prayer.

Lord, this is difficult work. Give me wisdom as I make very challenging suggestions. Help me offer Terri the proper understanding and support as she grieves the losses in her marriage and considers choices she might make to gain a healthier relationship.

"I know I can't live like this any longer," Terri continued. "I'm depressed—and I'm really tired of it. I don't want to keep drinking to cope with my pain. I want to lose weight, get back into church, and set some boundaries with Ken. So, yes, I'm willing to do whatever is necessary to give my marriage a chance."

Let's take a closer look at Terri and Ken's life through the perspectives of two authors who have profiled relationships in trouble. In my book *Love Lost: Living Beyond a Broken Marriage,* I referred to Dr. John Gottman and his research on marriages in crisis. Gottman, in *Why Marriages Succeed or Fail,* identifies "Four Horsemen of the Apocalypse"—the key symptoms that tell us a marriage is in trouble. As we look at each of these, consider which might be present in your marriage today.

The First Horseman: Criticism

Gottman says the first ugly horseman that will erode love and respect in a marriage is *criticism.* It "involves attacking someone's personality or character, rather than a specific behavior, usually with blame." Terri made her decision to demand change in their marriage, but when she confronted Ken about specific issues, he countered with an attack on her character. She also sometimes slipped into being overly critical of him, a symptom of her underlying anger.

The most damaging criticism often uses words like *always* and *never.* When Terri offered a complaint, Ken often rallied with something like this: "You're always criticizing me. I can never do anything right. Everything always has to be your way." As you might expect, responses like this created defensiveness, and Terri had to guard against joining in the mudslinging. As she reflected on their marriage, Terri realized that much of their conversation was filled with criticism and defensiveness.

Being critical is very different from offering a complaint, which is healthy in a relationship. Expressing appropriate anger and disagreement makes a relationship stronger in the long run. But according to Gottman, "The trouble begins if you feel that your complaints go unheeded (or if you never clearly express them) and your spouse just repeats the offending habits. Over time, it becomes more and more likely that your complaints will pick up steam."[1]

A complaint is a specific statement of anger or displeasure about a specific issue. Ideally, it offers a feeling statement and a specific request about what is needed to remedy the situation. A criticism is less specific and more global and often includes an attack on character.

A complaint could include saying, "I don't appreciate it when you leave your dirty towel laying on the bathroom floor. Would you mind picking it up after you shower?" A global, damaging criticism would be, "You always leave your towel on the floor like a slob. I don't know why you never pick up after yourself." You can see the dramatic difference between the two and the impact they would have on your mate.

Take a moment to do a quick check. Do you offer sincere statements that carry specific requests for change, or are your criticisms vague attacks on the other person's character? If you are firing criticisms instead of offering complaints, you can instigate a dramatic change in your relationship by communicating more constructively.

The Second Horseman: Contempt

A second major symptom to watch for in a troubled relationship is *contempt*. Gottman tells us that what separates contempt from criticism is *the intention to insult and psychologically abuse your partner.* "With your words and body language, you're lobbing insults right into the heart of your partner's sense of self. Fueling these contemptuous actions are negative thoughts about the partner—he or she is stupid, disgusting, incompetent, a fool. In direct or subtle fashion, that message gets across along with the criticism."[2]

In Terri and Ken's relationship, Terri heard the message from Ken that her opinions were ridiculous and without merit. Ken sometimes called her names when he was angry. He occasionally stormed out of the room, refusing to listen to her concerns.

Gottman tells us that when contempt is prevalent in a relationship, the positive qualities are forgotten. People only remember the angry outbursts, the hostile words, the mean-spirited, sarcastic comments. He says that couples must ban contemptuous comments from their relationship. A partnership has no room for words or body language that says, "You're stupid. I don't want to hear what you have to say."

Stop and think for a moment…has contempt invaded your marriage? Have you allowed contemptuous comments or body language to infiltrate your relationship? You may well feel resentment for certain issues in your marriage. But those feelings must not overrun every aspect of your marriage. You must be able to "contain" them, choosing carefully when, where, and how to have conflict. And remember the good things about your mate—don't let the anger contaminate other parts of your relationship. Can you recall the things you once admired in your mate? Dial those up again as you begin to rid your relationship of contemptuous behaviors.

The Third Horseman: Defensiveness

The third symptom to watch for in a troubled relationship is *defensiveness*. You can easily (and naturally) feel defensive when you believe your mate is attacking you. But defensiveness only makes things worse. And when the complaints are justified, defensiveness is a convenient way to avoid hearing the truth. Defensiveness—an attitude that says "I am not responsible for what you are accusing me of," or "I don't want to hear what you have to say"—only adds fuel to the fire.

Here are some signs of defensiveness to watch for in your relationship:

Denying responsibility. Regardless of your partner's complaint, you insist you are not responsible. You are not to blame for leaving your dirty clothes on the floor. You are not to blame for making an overdraft in the family checking account. Couples in trouble refuse to take responsibility for their failures and rarely apologize for them.

Making excuses. Who has not made excuses for wrong behavior? We might admit that we have done something wrong, but we're convinced the circumstances were out of our control. We couldn't get home on time because of traffic. We couldn't help care for the children because we didn't know what they needed. We overspent the checking account because no one told us the balance. Always a reason—always an excuse.

Cross-complaining. When your mate levels a criticism at you, you get even by dodging it and shooting back a similar complaint. If she accuses you of not helping with the children, you complain that she didn't help you the last time you disciplined the kids. If he accuses you of overspending, you deflect responsibility by pointing out that he did the same thing at another time.

Rubber man or rubber woman. In one slick move, you manage to dodge the accusation and accuse your mate of something entirely different. It is an adult version of the childhood game "I'm rubber, you're glue. Whatever you say bounces off me and sticks to you." In this game you skillfully find a way of making other people the focus of the problem, distracting them from their concerns about you.

Yes-butting. In this destructive version of defensiveness, you start by agreeing but then change course and steer the conversation away from the root of the problem. You might say that you are guilty of something but insist that you have a morally defensible reason for not doing what you were supposed to do. "Yes, I suppose you're right about me missing the performance with the kids, but I was so busy at work that I really couldn't make it," or "Yes, I lost my temper, but I've been working overtime for the family."

Take a moment to determine how much defensiveness exists in your relationship. Are you really open to hearing constructive complaints from your mate? Do you listen nondefensively, accept responsibility when appropriate, and work to find a solution to the problem? Consider how you can eradicate symptoms of defensiveness from your marriage.

The Fourth Horseman: Stonewalling

The fourth major symptom of trouble is *stonewalling*. This occurs when one partner decides to block out what their mate is saying. "You never say anything," Terri said to Ken recently. "You just sit there. I feel as if I'm talking to a brick wall." At times Ken might respond to a variation of this problem: "I can't say anything you'll listen to. It has to be your way or none at all. So I just shut up."

Gottman says that stonewallers often claim that they are trying to be neutral—to not make matters worse. "They do not realize that stonewalling itself is a very powerful act: it conveys disapproval, icy distance and smugness. It is very upsetting to speak to a stone-walling listener."[3]

Once either partner becomes a habitual stonewaller, the marriage is in trouble. One partner is likely to become overwhelmed by the mounting negativity.

Take a moment to decide if you or your mate is a stonewaller. Do you profess to listen without truly participating in the discussion? Do you simply wait for your mate to finish with the lecture, all the while tuning out the words? If so, make a note to work on this area.

These four patterns of interactions are devastating because they interfere with communication. They create a continuing cycle of discord and negativity that is hard to break. In fact, couples become so accustomed to this kind of interacting, they hardly notice it happening. Attack, defend, counterattack. The battle goes on and on until something explodes. After the smoke clears, the events may slowly escalate again.

If the Four Horsemen have been galloping through your relationship, they may cause another problem—you may be so busy firing and dodging criticisms that you never take time to call a cease-fire, apologize for inappropriate comments and responses, and reaffirm your appreciation of each other and your commitment to your relationship. Offer your complaints constructively, find a solution to the problem, and then move on to rebuild your relationship with words and actions that show you care.

At this stage of the process, we are identifying symptoms that hinder us from reaching our goal—an enjoyable and intimate relationship with our spouse. Don't let the Four Horsemen trample your love into the ground. Take note of them, herd them out of your conversations, and enjoy more open, honest, and constructive communication with each other.

2
Men, Women, and Stress

John Gray, author of the book *Men, Women and Relationships,* offers another window through which to view relationships. He identifies three "reactions to stress" for both men and women that provide clues that a marriage may be in trouble. Gray suggests that we need to consider and understand these symptoms so we can ensure they do not escalate into something worse in the relationship.

He Withdraws

Gray says that one of a man's first reactions to stress in a relationship is that he withdraws and detaches from the situation. When under stress, a man tends to deny his feelings and emotional pain. Obviously, when he withdraws, communication stops. Women, of course, become frustrated by this behavior and often take it personally.

Gray notes that the man not only stops communication but also becomes blind to pain. "He is unable to be compassionate. He minimizes the importance of problems that come up around him.

When his empathy is needed, he automatically withdraws to avoid feeling his own pain."[1]

People often accuse men of not taking women's feelings seriously. Although this may sometimes be the case, men are often simply overwhelmed by emotion. They are unable to process events and thus appear to be uninvolved. Of course, couples must navigate this problem in order to keep it from escalating into something more serious.

He Grumbles

When a man is stressed in his relationship, he grumbles. If someone asks him for help while he is in the middle of something else, he may resist and complain. If he is asked to change, he may grumble again. When a personal problem confronts him, he will grumble some more.

Gray says male resistance to change is related to a physiological difference between men and women. Women have more corpus callosum in their brains—the connective tissue that joins the right and left hemispheres of their brain. Because of this difference, women are able to access different parts of the brain more quickly. This makes them more flexible in their ability to shift goals in midstream.

The key here is that women should not take men's grumbling personally. The key for men is not allowing their complaining to escalate into a daily occurrence. If this becomes a habitual way of relating, the relationship may be in trouble. Of course, men must also get beyond the grumbling and into active problem solving. Issues do not evaporate with grumbling. Men must be challenged to "lean in" to issues—taking an active interest in the deeper problems present.

He Shuts Down

Gray says that the third way men typically respond to stress in a relationship is by shutting down. He says that this is an automatic reaction, not a conscious choice. Women generally feel that this reaction is a personal response, when in fact it is not. She imagines that he has some control over this reaction, but that is typically not the case. Gray notes that when a man is shutting down, he is simply asking for some space to process things. He is not rejecting her.

> In Native American tradition when a brave was upset, he would withdraw into his cave and no one was to follow. They understood that men under stress need to be alone. The brave needed to go inside and mull over the problem that was disturbing him. His squaw was warned that if she ran after him, she would be burned by the dragon that lived in the cave. The brave would come out when he was ready.[2]

We have discussed some of the typical reactions men have to stress and how they may interfere with a relationship. Let's now look at a woman's typical responses to stress and how they can lead to difficulties in a marriage.

She Becomes Overwhelmed

To the chagrin of many men, women tend to react to relational difficulties by becoming overwhelmed.

> If a woman is not used to being in touch with so much feeling, she is thrown out of balance and is unable to draw a clear line between her feelings and the feelings of others. She quite automatically feels an inner compulsion to respond not only to her feelings, but also to the feelings and needs of her partner and others.[3]

Unfortunately, a man doesn't often do well when his wife is overwhelmed. He tends to respond to her stress reaction with stress reactions of his own, which of course escalates things. To a simple request for help with a project, a woman might say, "I can't help you right now. I have clothes to wash, the house to clean, the kids to take care of. It's too much. I can't do it all." She is just stressed and trying to set boundaries, but if the man is not careful, he can take this personally.

She Overreacts

As a result of being overwhelmed, a woman moves into the second stress reaction—overreacting.

> In this state, an overreacting woman will tend to say things that are irrational, unfair, inconsistent and illogical—things that she will later on forget or say she did not mean. A few minutes later she may laugh about it. This is similar to the way a man responds under stress. He will become irritable and grumble, but if you don't resist him or take him wrong, it will quickly pass.[4]

Although her outburst may appear to hold him responsible for upsetting her, she probably did not mean to. She is in the process of sorting out what is bothering her. She may not know what is wrong, and like men, she needs time and space to figure things out.

She Becomes Exhausted

When a woman is upset and overwhelmed, she will probably become exhausted. She may feel temporarily depressed as if things are hopeless. Gray notes that a man's response is to feel threatened by his exhausted mate. He may take her exhaustion personally or believe that he has made her feel this way. He needs to realize that this is not his fault and that her feelings will pass.

Interestingly, Gray suggests that men have built-in pressure gauges that tell them when they are giving out more than they are receiving. He suggests that women do not have such gauges. In fact, the more stressed-out women feel, the more they forget about themselves.

Their solution to burnout is to center themselves by feeling that they are being heard and supported.

A Checklist of Symptoms

Let's take what we have learned from Drs. Gottman and Gray and see what symptoms parallel their reasons for concern. Perhaps as we apply this checklist to Terri and Ken, you can be doing the same for your relationship.

1. Do you find fault with your mate rather than finding solutions?
2. Do you analyze your mate's personality rather than focusing on the problem?
3. Do you make generalizations, using words such as *always* and *never* rather than being specific with concerns?
4. Do you feel resentment much of the time?
5. Do you use sarcasm or biting words when voicing complaints?
6. Do you have to be right when you and your mate argue?
7. Do you take responsibility for your part in marital problems?
8. Do you admire or appreciate some of your mate's characteristics?
9. Do you tend to be smug about your position?
10. Do you remember your mate's positive qualities when you're angry?
11. Do you really listen when your mate voices a complaint?
12. Do you acknowledge that you might be wrong when your mate voices a complaint?
13. Do you withdraw to avoid a big fight?

14. Do you withdraw because you feel overwhelmed by your mate's emotions?

15. Do you make irrational arguments?

Terri and Ken's marriage contains a mixture of troubling symptoms. Terri does not seem to overreact to Ken's tendency to stonewall—in fact, quite the opposite. She has gotten to the point where she can hardly respect anything about him. She feels resentment much of the time and may have a tendency to focus on personality traits rather than specific issues. She has struggled in her marriage for so long that she can barely remember anything good about Ken.

Looking at things from Ken's perspective gives us a different list of symptoms. He says that Terri overreacts to their problems and is smug in her opinions. He acknowledges that he withdraws to avoid a battle of words where he feels inadequate—a symptom common to many men. Although he agrees that their marriage is in trouble, he minimizes the level of the problem, and this infuriates her. She wants him to take their problems more seriously.

Both Terri and Ken agree that their communication, especially over heated issues, is nonproductive. Both admit that they easily slip into attack/counterattack maneuvers. They easily find fault with one another even though they know that causes pain.

Terri and Ken have also admitted they have let their spiritual lives grow weak and tepid. They would certainly benefit from renewing their commitment to Christ and to their former church. I have shared this passage with them for their encouragement:

> My purpose is that they may be encouraged in heart and united in love, so that they may have the full riches of complete understanding, in order that they may know the mystery of God, namely, Christ, in whom are hidden all the treasures of wisdom and knowledge (Colossians 2:2-3).

Terri and Ken are clearly in trouble. They are stuck in their well-worn dysfunctional patterns of interacting. Ken has made such a habit of interacting this way that he hardly knows anything different. Terri too has grown painfully accustomed to talking in these problematic ways. However, as her denial lessens, her anger increases. She has grown increasingly frustrated with their relationship, and now her e-motion—*energy in motion*—is leading her to create a crisis in their marriage. Sadly, couples rarely change until they face a crisis.

Living with Brokenness

I remember having a damaged bicycle when I was about ten years old. This J.C. Higgins bike worked, but only sporadically. I had to pedal cautiously to keep the chain from flying off, leaving me stranded alongside the road. I had somehow bent or broken a tooth on the sprocket that would sometimes accidentally send the chain flying off. My pedaling became a whir that produced no forward motion.

Sometimes the chain would only come partially off the sprocket—just enough to grab hold of my jeans and not let go. I would topple over into the brush on the side of the road, cursing and grumbling.

Perhaps you have been there—using baling wire and chewing gum to jury-rig a temporary solution, vowing to fix things correctly sometime in the future. I pounded and hammered that sprocket many times, always ending with the same poor results. I wanted to use shortcuts to make things work. I always told myself I would get around to fixing it properly some day.

How many of our marriages and other relationships are held together with baling wire and chewing gum? Are you using Elmer's Glue on your marriage, hoping against hope that the symptoms of distress will disappear? Perhaps you pray that things will magically heal, that your marriage will simply improve on its own. But it will not. Just as my bicycle did not repair itself without my attention, so too our marriages will not automatically repair themselves.

We must hear the terrible sound of the chain flying off, feel the powerlessness of our legs flailing about the pedals but providing absolutely no forward motion. We must admit that what we are doing, or not doing, is not working.

Denial will not help the situation. Our sprockets need repair. Only then will we enjoy riding along, using the power in our legs to create forward motion.

The writer to the Hebrews encourages us to free ourselves from the symptoms of brokenness and prepare to move forward.

> Therefore, since we are surrounded by such a great cloud of witnesses, let us throw off everything that hinders and the sin that so easily entangles, and let us run with perseverance the race marked out for us. Let us fix our eyes on Jesus, the author and perfecter of our faith (Hebrews 12:1-2).

These are powerful words to those of us—myself included—who prefer to live in denial. Along with the writer to the Hebrews, we must say, "Lord, free us from everything that hinders us from the free, exhilarating movement You desire for us."

In his later years, the apostle Peter wrote with a maturity he did not have as a young man. He encourages us to...

> prepare your minds for action; be self-controlled; set your hope on the grace to be given you when Jesus Christ is revealed… Just as he who called you is holy, so be holy in all you do… Now that you have purified yourselves by obeying the truth so that you have sincere love for your brothers, love one another deeply, from the heart (1 Peter 1:13,15,22).

Does your relationship have a broken sprocket? Do your jeans get caught in the chain, pulling you down in spite of your desire for things to work properly? Remember—if your actions are predictable, they're preventable. If you get on the same bike and the chain falls off every time, you might want to think about getting it fixed—and fixed right. If you are in a marriage and you feel the symptoms of brokenness, you might want to get to the doctor and get things fixed once and for all.

Checkup

Perhaps you have picked up this book because you wonder about the health of your relationship. Maybe you are past the point of wondering, and you know that your relationship is in trouble. You are struggling, feeling the pain that comes from a relationship fraught with tension and turmoil. You still have time to recognize and embrace your symptoms and take action. Denial, as you know, is not the answer. Sitting back and waiting for things to improve accomplishes nothing. Don't expect things to get better on their own. Troubled relationships rarely heal themselves spontaneously. Action is needed.

I strongly encourage you to embrace your symptoms and move forward to the next chapter, where we will talk about making an accurate diagnosis that will lead us to a remedy for your situation.

3
Where Did We Go Wrong?

The loggers came today—the squealing fan belt on their Ford Ranger announced their arrival. The truck was loaded with saws, axes, chain saws, and a gadget they called a come-along. Eric said it was "absolutely necessary for yarding the good wood."

Eric and his partner had come to clean out some fallen trees on my mountain property.

Dressed in flannel shirts and stained, patched jeans, they looked like loggers. Eric's face was craggy, showing the wear and tear of hard years outdoors. His sidekick, John, looked his part too, with the ponytail hanging out the back of his well-worn ball cap. John responded quickly to Eric's orders.

"We're ready to work," Eric said. "We'll yard 'em out, buck 'em up, load 'em up, and be out of here. We'll buzz up some of the other downed timber that's a little punky around the edges. It'll make good firewood. You'll be happy."

"Sounds good to me," I said. "Just don't leave a mess."

Eric looked at me as if I had hurt his feelings.

"I don't leave no messes on my projects," he said. "I'll build a small fire and burn the brush. I'm a certified forester, ya know. You'll be a happy camper when I'm done."

"As long as there's no mess, and I get two cords of firewood."

Eric put his hands on his hips, obviously annoyed by my comments.

"Look," he said. "You're getting a good deal, and you'll be happy with my work. You're going to like the firewood we leave for you. No worries."

I motioned for Eric to proceed and said we'd talk more after he got into the project.

By the end of the day, Eric had cut several trees into 16-foot lengths to be taken to a nearby sawmill. He was pleased with his work and, true to his word, had run a clean operation. Before leaving, he came and tapped at the door.

"Hey," I said. "How are things going?"

"Good," he said. "But you've got problems."

"What do you mean?"

"You have some sick trees. Come and look."

I followed Eric to a stand of firs next to my home. They looked healthy to me.

"Look closely at the tops. They're saying, 'Owie, owie.'"

I looked but still didn't see any signs of sickness.

"What am I looking for, Eric?"

By now, I was wondering if he was trying to find a way to get more timber off my property. The trees looked perfectly healthy.

"Look closer. The needles near the top are turning brown. The two trees on the left have some kind of fungus or bacteria and are dying. If you don't cut them down, they'll either come down in the next big blow or the disease will spread to other trees. I'd cut 'em down, but it's up to you."

A closer inspection revealed that Eric was telling the truth. The trees did look unhealthy. The lower limbs had already fallen off, and the needles on the upper limbs were turning brown, a sure sign that the trees were dying.

"What do you recommend?" I asked, hoping he might offer a less drastic course of action.

"I already told you. Take 'em down now or wait and watch 'em crash during a storm. Who knows how they'll fall. They look good on the outside, but inside they're probably punky all the way through."

I was shocked. These majestic trees had provided shade and protected me from the wind that whistled up the valley. Now my personal tree doctor had diagnosed them as sick and dying. Further, he'd suggested that if I didn't take action, the disease would spread, and the trees might fall during a storm, possibly damaging my home.

Hearing this news was difficult for me. Reluctantly, I decided to listen and have the trees removed. It was not an easy decision, but I had received an accurate diagnosis and needed to take the appropriate action.

Facing Your Pain

Accepting a diagnosis can be difficult. Perhaps, like so many of us, you don't like facing the truth. Perhaps you prefer to ignore the signs that your relationship is slowly dying and requires immediate action. But before you try to fix the problem, you must first find out how serious it is. You must decide whether the situation warrants intervention.

Michelle and Doug—a couple in their fifties—came to see me recently about problems with their relationship. Michelle, dressed sharply in a dark blue business suit, owned a local dress shop and carried herself with confidence. Doug, tall and sturdy with graying hair, was an accountant, and he dressed the part. Michelle immediately began sharing her concerns.

"We've been dating for a year, and it's time to make some choices.

I love him, but he's trying to control me. When I confront him, he says he'll stop, but then he goes right back at it. I'm not sure what I'm going to do."

"Doug," I asked, "what do you think?"

"I'm in the same place," he said. "I either want things to work, or else I think we should call it quits."

"So you're tired of living with things the way they are and want to change. You're the kind of couple I like to work with. Okay, let's dig in. I need to know some details about your relationship and what's not working."

Doug smiled at Michelle and reached out for her hand. They obviously cared for one another.

Michelle said, "We have lots of good things in our relationship, but some things aren't going well. I've been through two failed marriages, and I think I've learned some things."

"Let's hear your concerns, and then we'll give Doug a chance to respond. How does that sound to you, Doug?"

"Fine."

"Doug is very controlling with me," Michelle said. "We're not married, but he tells me how to spend my money. When I ask him to stop it, he tells me he's doing it for my own good. It makes me pull away from him, and then he gets more upset."

"How about it, Doug," I asked. "Sound familiar?"

"Yes, but that's not how I would describe things. I'm sharing my concerns about her spending. I'm an accountant. I think she should be thankful for my advice."

"So when you offer your assistance, she's receptive and thanks you, right?"

He noted my sarcasm.

"No, not quite," he said. "But I don't think she should pull away and punish me with silence."

I could see Michelle bristle.

"I push away because you try to control me. I don't want to talk to you when you ignore my requests to stop. You're not sensitive to my feelings."

"See what I mean?" Doug said, looking to me for help. "You can't tell me it's good for her to back away and stop talking to me just because I'm trying to help."

Here was a couple ready to abandon their relationship because they could not find a solution that worked for both of them. I watched as their affection for one another quickly gave way to anger and distance.

"I'm glad both of you recognize things are not working. You're listening to your symptoms and have come for help. Believe it or not, many couples suffer for years without seeking help. You're in a great position to make some important changes. Together we can diagnose the problems and talk about adjustments that need to be made."

Our work was cut out for us, but Doug and Michelle indicated they wanted to work together to solve their problems.

Why Does It Hurt So Bad?

Sometimes looking at someone else's relationship and observing what's going wrong is easier than seeing the same problems in our own. Let's consider Doug and Michelle's relationship for a moment. What is happening in their relationship that might be similar to your own?

Control

First, *Doug tries to control Michelle.* Doug has a history of trying to make Michelle manage money his way, which only makes her turn away from him. His effort to control her not only doesn't work, it makes matters worse. Even when she is ready to scream at him in frustration, he still seems insensitive to her concerns.

Many relationships suffer because one person tries to control another. People think theirs is the right way to do things, but their actions only make matters worse. No one wants to be controlled. People don't want their mate to tell them how they ought to do things. This type of communication never works. In fact, it's a sign of a relationship in distress.

Many couples use control in a moral context—they try to make the other person feel guilty for doing things a certain way. Their conversation is laced with words like *should* and *ought* and *the right way*. This implies that the other person's actions are wrong or bad. They do not simply offer their perspective—instead, they moralize about it as if their partner is committing a cardinal sin. Not surprisingly, this approach does not bring closeness and cooperation but simply pits one person against another.

Coercion

Second, *Doug uses coercive language to get Michelle to see things his way.* Whether he is right or not is beside the point. He tries to manipulate her into seeing and doing things his way.

Another reason coercive language is so destructive is that it automatically makes the other person feel defensive. No one wants to be controlled or manipulated into thinking a certain way. When we feel as though we are under attack, we erect barriers and stop communicating.

I'm surprised at how often couples use coercive communication with one another. Many try to talk their mates into seeing things their way and even label their way "the right way." I know people who tell their mates how to eat, dress, sit in a chair, and any number of other inconsequential things. This is a sure sign of a relationship in distress.

Distance

Third, *Michelle acts out her feelings by distancing herself from Doug.* Understandably frustrated, she no longer feels safe enough to talk things out with him. Her feelings go underground. Because she does not feel she can discuss their problems safely, their relationship suffers. Intimacy wanes. She retreats to avoid another conflict.

Distance is a sure sign of a relationship in trouble. Distance occurs when one or both partners no longer feel safe enough to share their feelings. Every couple needs to create a "safe container" where they can share their feelings without being confronted with a defensive response. If this safe container is not kept sacred, intimacy will surely diminish.

Taking Differences Personally

Fourth, *they take their conflicting opinions personally.* In this case, Doug seems to take Michelle's disagreement with him as a personal affront. He pushes and pushes, trying to get her to see things his way. In the process, she backs away from him, further intensifying his pain. In her own way, Michelle does the same thing—she takes his opinions personally without trying to negotiate with him.

Every therapist counsels about the importance of not taking conflict personally. It is a fundamental skill necessary in every relationship. And those who fail to master it will invariably struggle. Listen to Dr. David Viscott's counsel in his book *I Love You, Let's Work It Out*:

> Listen. Observe. Try to understand. Avoid retaliating in any way. Remind yourself that everything negative that is being expressed is one less thing to get in the way of feeling good. See the expression of feelings as relieving pressure. Be glad for the discussion, even if it makes you uneasy. And when your partner is finished, be still and allow room for more to be expressed. Don't jump right in. Keep listening.[1]

Viscott's counsel is important. He tells us that couples must not let negative feelings well up inside, creating resentment. Rather, they must harness feelings of resentment and use them for motivation to solve problems and bring about closeness.

Several powerful techniques have been particularly useful in my counseling practice as well as my personal life. You can use these techniques to lessen defensiveness and promote healthy conflict resolution.

Listen and *learn*. Don't *defend* and *debate*. This is a simple formula that can deliver dramatic results. We all need to listen to our mates and try to understand where they are coming from. Why are they saying what they are saying? What makes them think the way they do? Inquire. Probe. Explore. Seek more information. Don't defend yourself against their comments. This only fuels the fire. Instead, understand that their reaction is a comment about *them*, not necessarily about *you*. Again, *don't take things personally*.

Recently, this lesson hit home with me in a powerful way. My fiancée, Christie, had been harboring negative feelings because she thought I didn't want to spend time with her oldest son. In fact, I had said something about not having the best time when with him in the past, and I had forgotten having said it.

When Christie said she was hurt by my comment, I was immediately defensive. I defended myself by saying that her perception was not true. Our conversation became heated, and she suggested we take a time-out, which is always a good strategy. When we took up the subject again, I remembered my own counsel. *Settle down. Listen to her. See how she views things. Learn what she feels and wants.* As soon as I did this, she shared how my comments some time back had touched a nerve, and she invited me to share my current view—that I wanted to spend time with her son and recognized his importance in our lives. Issue settled.

Negotiating

Fifth, *Michelle and Doug no longer negotiate with one another.* Rather than cooperating to find a solution that works for both of them, Doug and Michelle are locked in a power struggle. Perhaps Doug's suggestions are worthy of Michelle's consideration. However, at this point, she has set her heart against him. Their relationship seems to include very little give-and-take.

The Scriptures consistently encourage us to be humble and to seek peace with one another. They teach us to guard against viewing our opinions too highly. The apostle Paul begs us to be reconciled to one another:

> As a prisoner for the Lord, then, I urge you to live a life worthy of the calling you have received. Be completely humble and gentle; be patient, bearing with one another in love. Make every effort to keep the unity of the Spirit through the bond of peace (Ephesians 4:1-3).

Peacekeepers strive for unity. They "make every effort" to be peaceful. They keep no record of wrongs, and they seek ways to reconcile themselves to each other. Doug and Michelle have set themselves against one another, and we can only hope their hearts will soften. They will need to learn to negotiate if they are to bring unity to their relationship.

Get Real

A diagnosis can bring many different reactions. When Eric diagnosed my fir trees, I cycled through a series of responses. At first, I was skeptical. Could these beautiful trees really be that sick? I explored the possibilities and decided to look more closely at the problem. Yes, in fact, the "doctor" appeared to be telling me the truth. I then had to embrace the diagnosis and take action. This was not easy for me, so I took several days to heed Eric's advice.

The counseling process almost always includes an awkward time, just after a couple comes to see me, when they must decide whether or not to embrace my diagnosis. If they do, we move forward into the hard work of behavior modification—changing patterns of interaction that will help their relationship. On the other hand, some couples refuse to accept the diagnosis. They are not ready to embrace change—it is simply too threatening for them. They are not prepared to relinquish partial control over their lives. They want to do things the way they always have done them rather than face the possibility of change.

Diagnosing Doug and Michelle's problems was a simple matter. Their dysfunctional patterns of relating were obvious to an outside observer. You and I have the benefit of standing outside their relationship. The view is not so clear for them. They are on the inside of things, plagued by the myopia that comes from being too close to the trees to see the forest.

Doug and Michelle decided to embrace my diagnosis. They decided to trust my experience and consider my perception of their problems. Trusting the diagnosis will be a challenge you will face as well. You may need to go through the process of relinquishing some control over your life to an expert who can provide necessary counsel.

The choice will be yours: Will you trust the counsel of someone who offers a diagnosis of your relationship? Will you trust his or her remedy for healthy relating?

4

When Trying to Help
Just Makes Things Worse

Diagnosing and fixing dysfunctional patterns of relating is some-times easy, sometimes not. I've found that overcoming most problems requires hard work.

Just as the medical doctor uses the stethoscope to listen care-fully to the functioning of the heart and lungs, we must use our eyes and ears to determine what is happening in our relationships. Only a discerning eye can recognize which patterns of interacting are healthy and which ones will cause only hurt and pain.

Couples in distress use several other strategies that never work. In fact, these strategies are certain signs of a relationship in trouble. As we move through this list, consider whether you and your mate exhibit these behaviors. This will enable you to make an accurate diagnosis and to make corrections.

Disagreeing and Arguing

Yes, it is that simple. If your mate makes a point and your first response is to disagree with it or argue about it, you will often end up deeper in trouble. If your mate is angry with you and you respond by pointing out some loophole in his or her argument, you are destined to make things worse. You can watch a predictable pattern emerge: She makes a point, and he disagrees with it. She escalates her position, and he escalates things even more by arguing with her.

Let's consider Doug and Michelle again. Doug tries to control Michelle's spending, and she responds by saying that she prefers not to be told what to do with her money. He then disagrees with her and becomes argumentative. Both escalate their arguing until she finally clams up and distances herself from him.

They need *understanding*. Michelle needs to let Doug know that she understands and even respects his knowledge of the matter. Doug needs to understand that Michelle is not going to necessarily do things his way regardless of his expertise. Arguing only leads to a lose-lose power struggle.

I am not saying that we must always agree with our mate. That would be ridiculous. A relationship consists of two different people from two different backgrounds, so we should not believe we will think alike about everything. However, rather than spend our time disagreeing with one another, we need to find the common ground in the relationship and capitalize on that.

Criticizing

Someone has said that every relationship starts with an *ideal* that transitions into an *ordeal* that creates a desire for a *new deal*. How true that is! Excessive criticism is often the indicator that someone is ready for a new deal.

Scott Peck, in his book *The Road Less Traveled,* says that the experience of falling in love is temporary:

> No matter whom we fall in love with, we sooner or later fall out of love if the relationship continues long enough. This is not to say that we invariably cease loving the person with whom we fell in love. But it is to say that the feeling of ecstatic lovingness that characterizes the

experience of falling in love always passes. The honeymoon always ends. The bloom of romance fades.[1]

After the bliss of early love, something changes.

What concerns me is what happens after the thorns on the rose appear. Most relationships can handle the fading of the rosiness of their relationship—but when the thorns become more noticeable than the petals of the rose and criticisms are more common than admiration, trouble is ahead.

Consider Michelle and Doug. He seems focused on Michelle's spending as if it were the sum total (no pun intended) of their relationship. His criticism of her has taken over their relationship. What happened to the discussions about other wonderful matters that brought them together in the first place? Why are they not spending their time talking about which play they wish to see or what new restaurant they will visit? When the wonder is eclipsed by criticism, serious trouble is not far away.

Winning

Relationships in trouble are made of individuals intent upon keeping score—and winning. You know the feeling. An issue comes to the forefront, and you want to prove you're right. You know in your gut that you're right and can prove the other person wrong. You see the error in your mate's ways and want to point it out. In short, you want to win.

Couples who fall prey to this kind of thinking are in big trouble because anyone in a power struggle who wins also loses. Anytime you engage in a battle with your mate and win that battle, you lose. Let me explain.

You are in a serious relationship or marriage, and you present your point of view. Because it is your *personal* point of view, you have some investment in it. You comment that the pastor gave a great sermon that touched your heart. You thought he spoke clearly and convincingly about a passage of Scripture. But your mate disagrees and sets out to prove that the pastor not only failed to offer a clear and convincing sermon but in fact rambled through the text and was thoroughly unprepared.

Now, having shared your heart and been vulnerable about your feelings, how will you feel when your mate picks your beliefs apart piece by piece? Being human, you will feel defensive and hurt. You may try to avoid taking the criticism personally, but that's tough to do. You will probably either clam up, feeling utterly defeated, or argue back, leading to a lose-lose exchange. This emotional trap is not easy to escape. The issue is clear: When we attempt to win in a relationship, we lose.

Being Passive-Aggressive

Passive-aggressiveness can take many forms, from "forgetting" something that is important to your mate to biting sarcasm. It may take the guise of ignoring your mate's request for change or sneering at a suggestion. Passive-aggressiveness is *any indirect expression of anger that is hurtful to your mate.* In short, it is a way to get even and express anger without taking responsibility for your anger or aggression.

As you review this list of concerns for relationships in trouble, you will notice many different forms of passive-aggressive behaviors. Indirect expression of aggression is a primary culprit in broken relationships. Pushing issues underground, pouting to avoid expressing anger, using sarcasm—all passive-aggressive. Couples who cannot compassionately and honestly discuss issues will find themselves fighting hidden, silent saboteurs of their relationship.

Complaining

Consider whether your relationship is fraught with complaints. Your mate may interpret these as "Nothing you do is ever good enough." (Its twin is *perfectionism.*) Being disappointed by various issues or character traits in a relationship is common. However, complaints must be offered sparingly, for they can erode your harmony and goodwill.

My adolescent son, Joshua, came to me and announced, "Dad, I don't think you ever want me to be happy or have fun."

I had always seen myself as a playful father and was flabbergasted by his comment.

"Why do you say that, Joshua?" I asked.

"Because every night when you come home, the first thing you do is complain about something. Tonight, the first thing you asked me was why my bike was left in the yard. Then you asked about my jacket on the couch and my tennis racket on the chair in the kitchen. If I listened to every one of your complaints, I'd be running around all night taking care of things."

I was speechless because what he said was true.

Every complaint I made about him was legitimate. He had left his bike in the yard, when he knew we preferred that he put it away. He had laid his jacket on the couch instead of hanging it up in his closet. His tennis racket was in the kitchen rather than in the toy rack in the garage. And to make matters worse, I could have complained about *even more things*.

What's the answer? Joshua had many issues that we needed to address, but he resented my criticism, and his spirit and his affection for me were weakened. I had created a family system where *rules* were more important than *relationship*.

In your relationship, are rules and complaints more common than praise and encouragement? Is the tapestry of your relationship threaded with complaints and hints of perfectionism or even control?

Listen to the apostle Paul concerning this issue: "Do not let any unwholesome talk come out of your mouths, but only what is helpful for building others up according to their needs, that it may benefit those who listen" (Ephesians 4:29).

My words certainly did nothing to build up my son. Instead, they were creating resentment and distance. I could win the battle of the wills, making him put away his bike, tennis racket, and jacket, but he would respond by withdrawing every time he heard my car pull into the driveway. Most importantly, he would never learn tolerance, kindness, gentleness, and patience.

Selfishness

Mature relationships have a quality I refer to as *mutuality.* They include a sense of giving back and forth, with each person being sensitive to meeting the other's needs. The opposite of this is, of course, selfishness—seeking your own way.

Far too often in my counseling practice I see women who complain that they carry 90 percent of the responsibility of caring for the children, maintaining the home, and promoting healthy communication in the family. Too often, men abdicate their familial and relational responsibilities, and women grow more and more resentful. Where is the give-and-take?

The apostle Paul gives more advice: "Serve one another in love." This implies that we are to listen to our mates' needs and meet them. We can relinquish our rights and let issues go. We are to be sensitive to our mates' concerns and work together to resolve them. The relationship includes *reciprocity,* and without it there is usually trouble.

Does your relationship have enough give-and-take? Do you stretch yourself to meet your mate's needs? Do you even know what they are? If you're not sure how you are doing in this area, ask your mate for feedback, but be ready for an honest reply.

Avoiding Spiritual Matters

Too many couples share a home, meals, and dreams with one another, yet they live miles apart spiritually. Couples in trouble often avoid spiritual matters. And yet if couples ever needed guidance from God, it is especially when they are hurting.

Consider Solomon's words about the importance of seeking wisdom from God:

> If you accept my words
>> and store up my commands within you,
> turning your ear to wisdom
>> and applying your heart to understanding,
> and if you call out for insight
>> and cry aloud for understanding,
> and if you look for it as for silver
>> and search for it as for hidden treasure,
> then you will understand the fear of the LORD
>> and find the knowledge of God (Proverbs 2:1-5).

Catastrophizing

Undoubtedly you know people who seem to insist on making a mountain out of a molehill. Subsequently, they live in chaos. Everything is a big deal. These people are often unhappy and seem to thrive on fighting and arguing about things. Sadly, this response to unhappiness only breeds greater misery.

People in healthy relationships work to keep everything in perspective. This may be as much an art as a skill. Sometimes I feel completely incapable of doing it myself; other times I am able to remember that God numbers the hairs on my head and sees every sparrow fall. Surely, this God, this all-knowing, all-seeing, loving God, can help me manage the complexities of my life. Surely, this Father God will help me when I feel as if I'm carrying the weight of the world on my shoulders.

This is a time to practice the old saying, "Let go and let God." Remember that God "has made everything beautiful in its time" (Ecclesiastes 3:11).

Lack of Self-Control

Our final diagnostic indicator is perhaps the greatest common denominator of relationships in trouble—the *lack of self-control*. As you read the following examples, consider the accompanying lack of self-control. In each and every one of the symptoms, a lack of self-control is evident—allowing oneself to behave in ways that are self-destructive and damaging to the relationship.

Every day I receive letters from couples in distress who desperately want healing in their relationships. I commonly receive the following complaints and hear about these symptoms of turmoil:

- My husband secretly views pornography even after he has promised to quit.
- My wife had an affair.
- My husband has an anger problem and refuses to get help for it.
- My husband is addicted to online gaming and won't stop.
- My wife continues to spend money well beyond our agreed-upon limit.
- My husband won't attend church with our family anymore.
- My wife is too harsh with our children.
- My husband acts gentle and loving in church, but he's aggressive and angry at home.

Perhaps some of these examples hit close to home for you. In each of them you can see the issue of *immaturity*. Each of the problems is emotional as well as spiritual.

Peter offered a radical recommendation to Christians:

> Therefore, prepare your minds for action; be self-controlled; set your hope fully on the grace to be given

you when Jesus Christ is revealed. As obedient children,
do not conform to the evil desires you had when you
lived in ignorance. But just as he who called you is holy,
so be holy in all you do (1 Peter 1:13-15).

Peter is saying that as obedient children of Christ, we are called
to a higher standard—one of self-control and holiness. Although we
may be tempted to complain, argue with one another, lie, coerce, and
cheat, these are no longer options. God calls us to a life of spiritual
and emotional maturity.

The Power of Diagnosis

I have always had an intense ambivalence about the word *diagnosis*. It holds such power—the power to send me into anxious
fretting and the power to drain away worry from every taut muscle
with a giant *ahhh*.

Recently, I felt some intense and prolonged discomfort in my
stomach. I gulped Pepto-Bismol, hoping to eliminate the pain. The
pain persisted, and I decided to see my doctor.

I usually put off seeing my doctor (or dentist) until I have two
or three complaints to talk about.

Sitting in the waiting room, I felt all the ambivalence newcomers
often express when awaiting their initial counseling appointment
with me. *Is this really that important?* I mused. *Couldn't it have waited
until the symptoms disappeared on their own?*

"David Hawkins?" the nurse called.

I jumped up, heading for the door she held open.

She gestured for me to enter an examining room. "Sit down and
take off your shirt," she said, offering a faint smile. She looked too
young to be a nurse.

"The doctor will be right in," she said.

I busied myself with a magazine. I tried to ignore my pain and
the cold examining table, but I needed a diagnosis—and a remedy.

After a few minutes, Dr. Butler came in, reading my chart and examining the symptoms I had described to the nurse. Middle-aged, he looked like a TV doctor—tall and lanky, with white hair and a Lincolnesque beard. He wore a lab coat with his name printed on it, evoking confidence and power. The power of diagnosis.

"So, what seems to be the problem?"

"I've been having stomach problems for several days," I said.

"Show me exactly where it hurts."

I pointed to the place on my abdomen where the pain originated.

He began poking and probing, as if searching for an enemy by Braille. I gasped as he put pressure on the sore areas.

"Not your appendix. That's good news. It's your lower intestine. Any nausea?"

"Some."

"Probably a virus that has settled into your lower stomach. Have you taken any over-the-counter medicine?"

"Pepto-Bismol."

"Has it helped?"

"No."

"That won't work on a virus. We'll give you something stronger, and if that doesn't do it, I want to see you again tomorrow."

"Thanks, Dr. Butler," I said, forcing a smile. Was this all there was to it? No dreaded stomach cancer, no thorough workup, no CAT scan?

Indeed, after a sound sleep and appropriate medication, I was much better the next day. Dr. Butler made a quick and accurate diagnosis. Symptoms—diagnosis—remedy. *Ahhh*.

Relationship Distress Checklist

The time has come for you to perform an examination of your relationship. Consider the ineffective strategies we have discussed in this chapter and determine which ones exist in your relationship. Use this checklist to diagnose the trouble you are experiencing.

- Do you argue so much that you feel discouraged?
- Does your mate try to change your feelings and thoughts rather than understand them?
- Do you or your mate criticize too often?
- Do you or your mate act passive-aggressively with one another?
- Do you have enough give-and-take in your relationship?
- Do you and your mate avoid discussing spiritual matters?
- Do you or your mate tend to complain a lot about the relationship?
- Do you or your mate tend to blow problems out of proportion in the relationship?
- Do you and your mate have power struggles?
- Do you feel unsafe with your mate? And as a result, do you avoid talking about certain "hot topics" in your relationship?
- Do you feel a lack of self-control in your relationship?
- Do you fail to reach agreements that will solve problems?

If you answered yes to at least two of the questions above, you have reason for concern. If you answered yes to four or more questions, you need immediate help.

Checkup

Just as no one has a perfect body, no one has a perfect relationship. So don't be discouraged if you did not receive a perfect score. In fact, if you did, you may be living with a hint of denial!

The questions on the previous page will help you and your mate check your emotional and spiritual pulse. Remember that just as you go to your medical doctor for medical advice, you are reading this book for emotional and spiritual advice. My hope is that the checklist will highlight areas of difficulty in your relationship, offering a place where you can begin to work together.

If you and your mate are truthful with one another, you probably know whether your relationship is in distress. Your answers will offer you a diagnosis that can lead to an appropriate remedy.

So let's get to it!

5

How to Heal
a Hurting Heart

Things naturally break down. People die, things are damaged or lost, and relationships fall apart.

Physicists have a word for this: *entropy*—the tendency for things to deteriorate over time. Because I know this to be a fact of life, I try to be philosophical when it happens. I'm fairly successful except when it hits too close to home.

Recently my laptop died. It offered a few symptoms of its impending demise. I was typing away, and suddenly the screen shivered and went blank. I was shocked. Where was my writing? Had it disappeared into some great technical abyss?

My beloved Gateway was only two years old. I had assumed we would be together for years!

At first I hoped its symptoms would magically abate. I ignored the danger signs, hoping the computer would rebound with a new spirit. Perhaps it was tired and would feel better after a good night's rest. I was hoping for spontaneous recovery—much like quarreling couples who believe they simply need a little time apart to get things straightened out.

I avoided seeing the computer doctor because… well, I was busy, and I was also in denial.

Extra "sleep" didn't cure my laptop, and I was finally forced to call a repairman. I handed him the laptop, saying I *really* needed the documents it contained (as though that would somehow make a difference).

"The symptoms you describe could point to a number of different things," he said. "I'll run some tests to see what's wrong."

"How bad can it be?" I asked.

"It could be something as simple as…" and there I lost him in his techno-talk. "Or your hard drive could be fried. By the way, did you *ever* leave your computer on while removing a disk drive?"

I felt my heart sink.

"Yes," I answered.

"You can *never* do that. It's a sure way to fry your hard drive or motherboard. I'll get back to you in a day or two."

"A day or two?" I said. "I use my computer every day."

"It's going to take some time to figure out what's wrong and fix it."

Returning two days later, the computer guy carried my laptop as if it were a corpse. I feared the worst.

"Your hard drive is damaged," he said, "but I was able to fix it."

"And the documents?"

"I restored your hard drive, and I think all your data is still there. But you've got to learn to back up your information on a regular basis. Computers can go bad without much warning. They're just machines."

The doctor's expertise had saved the patient. But not without a real scare. I took a deep breath and thanked him, vowing to take much better care of my laptop from this point forward.

Happy Endings Can Happen

Machines inevitably break down. Sometimes we can repair them, and sometimes we can't. Relationships have a tendency to break down as well, though I am always rooting for them to succeed, and I think most can. I'll admit that I also enjoy those sappy chick-flicks, especially the ones with the predictably warm and happy endings. One of my favorites is *You've Got Mail*. I can recount nearly every scene from this story of Meg Ryan and Tom Hanks' volatile relationship. Perhaps you remember the plot.

Ryan plays the friendly owner of a neighborhood bookstore in New York. She is young and perky and absolutely loves books. Hanks is her opposite—a ruthless scion of a book empire, intent on running her out of business.

Ryan does not go down without a fight. David takes on Goliath. But in this case, David loses. In spite of the encouragement and valiant support from family and friends, she is forced to close her shop.

Behind the drama of the corporation wiping out the local mom-and-pop store is a relationship that has developed through e-mail. Having met in a chat room, both are looking for meaningful conversation and find that they genuinely care for one another. On his laptop, Hanks is kind and tender. He listens to Ryan as she shares the pain of losing her beloved business, and because he doesn't know she is referring to her battle with him, he even offers tips on how to take on the mighty giant.

The daily conversations lead to romance. After significant initial hesitation, they decide to meet. Imagine their surprise to find they are attracted to "the enemy." As the music plays and spring flowers are in bloom, we see our couple meet and embrace in Central Park. How can you not cry at this poignant encounter? We see that love can flourish when acrimony is kept out of the picture. Even enemies can fall in love.

Although it is an unlikely story, it contains several applicable truths. I have seen many troubled couples rise like the phoenix from the ashes to again enjoy a dynamic, loving romance. I have seen couples on the edge of divorce build a bridge across the chasm of conflict to one another.

Unlikely, you say? That depends on your will to make it happen, your willingness to appropriate the power of God to change and transform your hearts.

This section of *The Relationship Doctor's Prescription for Healing a Hurting Relationship* offers tools for rebuilding your marriage, including strategies for healing old wounds and restoring the love you once had for one another.

How to Mend a Broken Heart

Perhaps this book finds you with a wounded heart. You knew the power of light-headed romance once, when you and your spouse first met and the two of you drank from the intoxicating well of love. But that was years ago. Those dizzy days are long gone, and now you look across the table at your mate and wonder if you ever really knew him or her at all. You suddenly hate the way he chews his food. You despise the way she sniffles at the first sign of a cold. Too often you don't enjoy or appreciate each other's company. What happened? Where did the love go? How has so much distance crept into your relationship?

The intervening years may have brought profound disappointments. Has unfaithfulness severed the sinews of your affection? Do addiction issues—alcohol, work, drugs, eating—tear at the very soul of your relationship? Perhaps online gaming or a chatroom dalliance has caused seemingly irreparable damage. Any of these factors can ruin a relationship, but you still have good reasons to hope for recovery. You can escape the pit of despair. Let's explore some of the ways together.

As we have learned in previous chapters, determining how things went wrong is important. But knowing where to go from there is even more critical. Anyone can bemoan the diagnosis, but we need courage to decide what to do about it. Let's consider some practical tools for healing a broken heart. Let's look ahead to the horizon and envision how you can restore your relationship.

Admit You Have Been Wounded

Denying your pain won't help. Don't feel bad for risking it all for love and coming up short. In fact, your willingness to take that risk is a wonderful trait. But if you are reading this book because you are hurt and want to find a way back to your loved one, you must first accept your pain. Look deep inside your heart and notice what is there.

You may be tempted to cover your pain with anger. People commonly place their sadness and hurt on the shelf and put on the tougher, more powerful feelings of anger and rage. Be careful. Anger, rage, and bitterness may feel more potent, but too often they lead to unpleasant changes. Your tender, softer self becomes a brittle tortoise shell that hides your vulnerable heart.

I remember the incredible loss I felt after the unwanted separation during my marriage. I vividly recall the cold winter morning when I looked at my wife, bags in hand and car loaded with boxes, and asked her one last time if the separation was necessary. I was filled with a profound sadness when she said, "Yes. This is what I want."

My sadness, however, soon gave way to anger and resentment. Sitting quietly with my grief was too painful. I wanted to feel more powerful, more in control of my destiny. The truth is, I wasn't strong enough to bear my pain. I don't know if forcing myself to tolerate my sadness and pain would have changed the outcome, but anger and resentment surely did little to build a healthy bridge between my wife and myself.

My reaction was not unique. Many of the people I counsel in similar circumstances would rather opt for powerful, ego-strutting anger than settle for fragile sadness and vulnerability. We want answers. We want movement. We want change. In fact, we demand them. We are an incredibly impatient bunch, and this impatience does nothing to help the healing process.

Counselors have long said, "A feeling denied is intensified," or "You have to feel it to heal it." These notions sound simplistic, but they're true. Allow yourself time to feel the wound that exists in your relationship today. But know that it is temporary. Remember that Solomon's wise counsel was to recognize "a time to weep and a time to laugh, a time to mourn and a time to dance" (Ecclesiastes 3:4). This season of pain and loss won't last forever. You will move forward. But being patient and "being with" your loss and pain can help you accelerate the process.

Be Open to New Answers

Notice that I said *new* answers. Check the common theme in the well-worn sayings below.

- If you do what you've always done, you'll get what you've always got.
- Doing the same thing and expecting different results is called insanity.
- A breakdown comes before a breakthrough.

These may sound trite and overly simplistic, but they contain powerful nuggets of truth that apply to our conversation. Are you willing to let this time of difficulty *work on you*? Are you willing to dig deep and look for answers? What you have been doing is not working. Doing the same old things and hoping for magical change is as foolish as me waiting for my computer to heal itself.

I receive e-mails and letters every day from people struggling in their relationships. These good people are intensely frustrated but unable to break free from their failed patterns of reacting. They hate the state of their current world, but they seem paralyzed to do anything different. They eagerly complain about their mates' behavior yet persist in their own.

A recent e-mail from Darla indicated just such a struggle.

Dear Dr. David. I need your help with my marriage. My husband is a leader in our church, but he leads a double life that no one knows about but me. He seems to be addicted to pornography. I have caught him looking at pornography on the Internet many times. I check his computer and often find new activity on X-rated sites. Each time, he apologizes and promises to quit. He stops for a while, and then I catch him at it again. We have been through this cycle many times. I'm losing my trust and love for him. Each time I catch him, my heart sinks, and I pull away. He resents that and says I punish him even after he's said he's sorry. I'm ready to give up but don't believe in divorce. What can I do? Darla.

As we review Darla's letter, we can sense her desperation. When she confronts her husband, he apologizes and promises to change. Perhaps he means well, but he continues to repeat the pattern of destructive behavior. Sadly, we can see the fabric of their marriage disintegrating. Darla will call it quits pretty soon—at least if *she* keeps doing what she has done. She seems just as caught up in the vicious circle as her husband. She seems bound to a series of reactions: Investigate his actions, become angry and discouraged, accept his apology, start the cycle over again.

Even though this approach has not been successful, she has not tried anything new. She has apparently not gone to counseling and has not sought their pastor's intervention. She has not brought his secret sin to light. Subsequently, he has little accountability, and she can expect little change. Talking to the pastor might not force change, but not bringing the problem to light enables it to continue.

We must be open to new answers. We must bathe our concerns in prayer, seek answers and insights, and be ready to apply counsel. Tragically, Darla is living the classic mistake: She's doing the same things and expecting different results. It simply doesn't work!

Listen to these words of Solomon concerning the search for wisdom.

> If you call aloud for insight
>> and cry aloud for understanding,
> and if you look for it as silver
>> and search for it as for hidden treasure,
> then you will understand the fear of the LORD
>> and find the knowledge of God (Proverbs 2:3-5).

Insight, understanding, and wisdom can lead to profound remedies for problems.

Seek God and Allow Him to Work in You

Another powerful tool for restoring relationships is our humble cry for insight. In our brokenness, we realize that our actions are only making matters worse. Once we accept this, we are much more likely to seek God's help. We search for insight and understanding as for hidden treasure. This takes work.

At one time, I was an avid fisherman. I spent many Saturdays during my high school summers searching out the perfect fishing holes with my buddies. With dogged determination, we climbed over brushy hillsides, scraping ourselves up in the process, to get to a ravine where a creek washed through. No other fishermen were in sight. After hours of hiking, we cast our lines into these pristine pools and hooked our fill of brook trout. The hike and the scrapes were well worth the toil and trouble.

Are you willing to do some strenuous hiking to find answers to the brokenness you feel in your relationship? Are you willing to search for books on the topic? Seek expert counsel? Examine the Scriptures? If so, I am confident that you will find answers to your problems.

In the Sermon on the Mount, Jesus offers some startling advice—He tells the crowd not to worry about their lives—about their bodies, what they will eat or drink, or what they will wear. "Look at the birds of the air; they do not sow or reap or store away in barns, and yet your heavenly Father feeds them. Are you not much more valuable than they? Who of you by worrying can add a single hour to his life?" (Matthew 6:26-27).

He goes on to offer a new perspective, and His counsel is relevant to our discussion about broken relationships as well.

"But seek first his kingdom and his righteousness, and all these things will be given to you as well. Therefore, do not worry about tomorrow, for tomorrow will worry about itself. Each day has enough trouble of its own" (6:33-34). There it is—if we seek God, we find Him. And we find the answers we are looking for as well.

Work on Changing the Relationship—and Yourself

This is where we come to the application of the new principles. You must allow God's wisdom, along with the practical tools you have learned, to take root. You place yourself under God's gracious healing hand. You are receptive to what He is trying to teach you.

"For the word of God is living and active. Sharper than any two-edged sword, it penetrates even to dividing soul and spirit, joints and marrow; it judges the thoughts and attitudes of the heart" (Hebrews 4:12).

The word of God is potent medicine. I confess that I cannot fully understand the power of the Scripture, but I surely believe it. I believe that if I immerse myself in the Scriptures, they will change me. I believe they are capable of showing me things I never saw before. Are you willing to listen to what God has to say about your broken relationship?

You must not only listen to the word of God and consider what it says about your life, you must also *apply it*. This may be the hardest part. Consider these possibilities:

- Perhaps you need to humble yourself with your mate.
- Perhaps you need to give up your right to certain things or ideas.

- Perhaps you have been using abusive language and need to stop.
- Perhaps you have addiction issues that require professional attention.
- Perhaps you need to apologize.
- Perhaps you need to make amends.
- Perhaps you to need to repent (turn away from something).
- Perhaps you need to seek for equality in your relationship.

As you look at the items above, consider which fit your current situation. What changes is the Lord asking you to make?

Seek Support

Restoring your relationship can feel like lonely work. Relationship struggles can be terribly isolating. You will do well to find support during these difficult times.

You may feel too embarrassed to seek counsel. You may feel vulnerable going to your pastor and admitting that things are not perfect. Remember, you are not alone. Anyone who has dared to be in a relationship knows the pain of a relationship in trouble. Anyone who has risked caring deeply for another knows the anguish of a heart broken. These things happen to everyone at one time or another. But you can soften your pain and speed your recovery by reaching out for support.

A few words of caution. Finding support does not mean enlisting a friend to help you criticize your mate. If you talk your friend into taking up the offense against your partner, you will have gained nothing. You may feel temporarily vindicated, but you won't be building a bridge back to your mate. Having a friend commiserate with you soothes wounds temporarily but does little to create healing.

Choose your confidants carefully. Can you trust them to offer sound, unbiased counsel? Will they be willing to tell you the truth about your own behavior? Can they empathize without becoming embroiled in the struggle? Are they mature, and do they supply wise counsel?

Support may come in the form of professional help. Why professional support? Because without a third party to help you see what you are doing to one another, you are much more likely to repeat destructive patterns. You may need someone to confront you about behaviors that are damaging your relationship.

In this book, I have purposefully used medical analogies to make the point that marital health, like physical health, requires our full attention. Consider how you might feel in the following scenario:

You have suffered a piercing stomachache for two days. Pepto-Bismol and antacids have provided no relief from the vomiting and sleeplessness. Finally, you tire of the pain, and in desperation, you make an appointment with your doctor. You convince the appointment manager to fit you in that afternoon.

As you sit in the office, waiting your turn, your stomach continues to ache, and you worry about the possibility of an ulcer, appendicitis, or even worse—stomach cancer. Focused on your pain, you barely hear your name called. You jump up and rush into the doctor's office, where the nurse takes your vital signs. The doctor finally comes in, asks a few questions, and without even conducting an exam, says, "You're fine. I think it's just a bug that is going around. If you're not better in a few days, come back and see me."

If this happened, I'm sure you would be shocked. At the very least, you would seek a second opinion. Yet, the way this doctor responded is too often they way we treat our emotional and relational problems. We take a couple of aspirin and hope things will be better in a year or two. This is not good emotional or relational care. Don't treat yourself this way—get appropriate help.

The State of the Relationship

When restoring a relationship, talking to your mate about how you are doing is critical. Although the news may not be good, and many issues may come to the table, the first step is to talk about them.

I suggest that you and your mate schedule times, preferably several days a week, to review how things are going. This is a time to share how the relationship is *from your perspective.* It is not a time to point fingers of blame but to simply state *how you feel, what you think,* and *what you want.* Make clear that everything you say is from your point of view and is not a statement of fact. Let me give you an example from a meeting with a couple I counseled recently.

Jack and Carolyn, both in their forties, have been married for 15 years and have three children, ages 14, 10, and 8. Jack is a solid man, slightly overweight, yet in good physical condition. He is dressed in jeans and a long-sleeved dress shirt. His full beard is beginning to gray. Carolyn is an attractive woman in fashionable slacks and blouse. Her long brown hair hangs to her shoulders. Both are friendly.

They agree that their marriage had been in great shape until Jack had an affair a year ago. This came as a terrible shock to Carolyn, who had thought their relationship was strong. She was deeply wounded by the affair and cannot get beyond the feelings of betrayal.

They came for counseling at Carolyn's insistence. She told me she had not seen the affair coming, and it broke her heart. She has always been faithful and has tried to meet her part of their relational needs. She shared that she had always worked on being a companion to Jack, cared for their home, and even encouraged the family to be involved in church. She thought their relationship was strong.

Jack, on the other hand, said he had been unhappy prior to the affair and had felt Carolyn pulling away from him emotionally. He agreed with her perception of caring for the children and home, but he did not feel her friendship. He said he had never felt special to her. Thus, he had sought other companionship, which eventually led to the affair.

Jack acknowledges that his actions were wrong, but he is impatient with Carolyn for taking so long to forgive him. She too feels impatient with her pain and wonders if she ought to be able to move on. After all, Jack is sorry for what he has done and vows not to repeat the behavior. Thus far, he has been true to his word.

I advise both that healing a wound of this nature takes time. It requires the creation of a "safe container" where Carolyn can emote by sharing feelings of rage, hurt, and sadness as she works through the betrayal. Jack will need to allow her these times of turmoil without becoming defensive and attacking her, which would only make matters worse. He too needs an opportunity to share his feelings of regret, sadness, and anger. He will need to explore his feelings of rejection from before the affair, and both Carolyn and Jack need to examine preexisting issues within the relationship.

We agreed Carolyn and Jack would have "state of the relationship" meetings twice a week. We set up the following rules:

- Each person is allowed ten minutes to talk about his or her feelings, thoughts, and desires.

- No attacking or hitting below the belt is allowed.

- The other person simply listens, offering answers if requested, without giving a defense.

- The other person practices not taking statements personally, remembering that the partner is sharing his or her own feelings and thoughts.

- After sharing, they will, if possible, agree on a plan of action for the next several days, which might involve some activity or additional time together.

Many couples have used the "state of the relationship" strategy at various stages of difficulty. Some couples are doing well and simply want a time to check in with each other. It is a great opportunity to *make contact*. In a busy world, with many distractions, a designated time to touch bases can be invaluable.

Just Do It

Made famous by the folks at Nike, this slogan can be an important remedy for broken relationships. A time comes when we just need to do it. If we have long been considering going on that diet and embracing healthy eating habits, the time is right to *just do it*. If you have considered making a daily Scripture reading part of your life, *just do it*. If your heart has been convicted by certain Scriptures that implore you to change, *just do it*.

I find that many people know what needs to be done. But they often need to hear themselves say it out loud. They need an audience to provide validation. But they know. Just as you know. If you have pondered God's words, if you have heard His advice, and if you have listened to your own wisdom, you know. Now it is time to *just do it*. Take a deep breath, hang on tight, and take action.

6
The Art of Communication

"You have to talk to each other," I told Jack and Carolyn. "There is no substitute for this. If you want your relationship to survive and thrive, you must spend time talking."

It seems like such logical, pragmatic counsel. This couple didn't need a psychologist to tell them that—or did they? Why do we all seem to require constant reminders that the most potent remedy for a broken relationship may be to keep the conversation flowing? The answer may have to do with the countless distractions and impediments that interrupt the natural and healthy flow of communication.

As you examine the following list of practical tools for healthy communication, consider your own relationship. How can you apply some of these simple tools to start the healing process?

Time

As you know, nothing can substitute for time spent with your mate. A man can bring his wife flowers, take her on expensive vacations, and buy her the BMW she has always wanted, but if he doesn't spend time with her, he will never have the relationship he desires.

John Eldridge, in his books *Wild at Heart* and *Captivating,* talks about the importance of a man pursuing his woman and a woman feeling this energy of her man pursuing her heart. A man needs a maiden to rescue, he says, and a woman needs to know that her man will go to great lengths to rescue her.

Think back to when your man or woman sought your affections. Remember the relentless pursuit of *you—just you.* You were the single focus; no other person was on the radar screen.

These dynamics are still necessary today. She still needs to know she is number one—ahead of work, play, friendships, and addictions. He needs to know she admires and appreciates him. In spite of all of our faults, we need to know that our partners will pursue us.

You can accomplish this easily—with focus. If you will take ten minutes every night to check in with one another, you will make a great start. If you have a date night once a week, you will add more to the positive energy between you and do much to dispel any negative feelings that have arisen. Take turns preparing a surprise element to the date night.

Richard Stuart, in his book *Helping Couples Change,* suggests having "Caring Days." He teaches husbands and wives to write down a list of positive, specific ways their partners can please them. A man might say, "I'd like you to give me a foot massage before bed at night." A woman might say, "I'd like you to read to me for fifteen minutes when we go to bed." The partners grant each other a certain number of these requests regardless of how they feel about each other. Those of you familiar with the 12-step program will recognize this as *fake it until you make it.* The great thing is that it works. It helps build better communication and positive feelings toward one another.

My fiancée and I enjoy a variation on this theme. We have a "dream jar," where we place slips of paper that describe activities we want to do together. We take turns picking an activity out of the jar. This has been a great way to share adventures. We've had wonderful trips to the ocean or the Olympic Mountains, as well as lunches or dinners in many of the quaint neighborhoods in Seattle. It is a wonderful way to break out of the routine and monotony of life.

Vulnerability

Spending time together is a start, but it does not guarantee intimacy. Two people sitting side by side in a rail car watching the most beautiful scenery may not share the adventure of togetherness if they do not speak a word.

Another ingredient is needed: *vulnerability*. This requires that you share intimately with one another. You practice the art of sharing how you feel, what you think, and what you want. Men, this means you will need to practice identifying and actually naming different feelings! "Good" is not a feeling. Neither is "fine." Learning our array of feelings (such as hurt, sad, encouraged, joyful, and excited) and sharing them is a powerful connector.

You may be experiencing significant trouble in your relationship, and sharing feelings may be the last thing you want to do. You would much rather blame your mate. You are inclined to attack and punish. This is not being vulnerable. Let me give you an example from Carolyn and Jack's relationship.

Sad and angry during a particular counseling session, Carolyn did not feel like affirming Jack. Rather, she wanted to explode on him. She wanted to say, "I hate you for what you've done. You've ruined everything. You are a rotten and selfish person." Instead of saying it, I counseled her to *speak from her most vulnerable self.* After a bit of rehearsal, Carolyn shared the following:

"Jack. I feel very raw today. All I can think about is you cheating on me. I feel betrayed. I can't understand how you could do this to me. It feels so personal. I feel weak and fragile as if my world has crumbled around me. I don't know who to trust. Part of me wants you to hold me, and another part doesn't want you to touch me."

When Carolyn shared this way—speaking from her most vulnerable self, rather than attacking—Jack was able to listen and empathize. She felt better having shared this with him, and he was able to comfort her rather than merely defend himself and push her away.

Listening

We can easily pretend to be listening. We may look our mates in the eye and nod our heads while we are busy creating our rebuttals. This is not listening.

Real listening demands our entire attention. It requires that we seek to fully understand where our mates are coming from. Why are they saying what they are saying? What do they need from us? What is unfinished in their hearts? Listening is not a passive process—it is very active.

A simple axiom may be helpful to you: Practice listening and learning instead of defending and debating. When you are engaged in a debate with your mate, you are not likely to be really listening. If you are thinking of all the ways you disagree or are considering how to defend your position, you are not listening. When you really listen, you validate your mate's right to his or her perception. Try it and notice the difference it makes.

Listening is one thing; *soulful listening* is another thing entirely. The difference is huge. Soulful listening involves hearing not only what is said but also what is not said. As Jack listens to Carolyn voice her feelings of despair, he has several choices. Does he just listen to her words and say he understands, when in fact he may not? Or does he help her find words for her feelings of discouragement and fragility? Soulful listening involves taking the next step—actually putting yourself in other people's shoes and helping them express what they may not yet be able to say. It is a powerful technique that will bring you much closer.

Forgiveness

You have been hurt. Words spoken in anger have struck raw nerves. "Once burned, twice shy," the saying goes. Now you guard your heart—and that is wise. But a guarded heart does not have to be unwilling to forgive and take chances again. It is simply cautious and discerning.

To risk relating is to risk having your heart broken. I do not want you to be reckless with your affections. Rather, I want you to consider what is best for you and your relationship and to pursue avenues of healing.

One of the surest forms of healing comes through the act of forgiveness. I use the word *act* cautiously because forgiveness comes in stages, many of which are repeated over and over again. Carolyn, for example, moved through the stages of grief (denial, anger, bargaining, sadness, acceptance) many times. Just when she thought she was on solid ground, a "sneaker wave" of grief would hit, sending her spiraling downward until she could catch her breath and regain her equilibrium. Forgiveness has been anything but a smooth ride for her.

Carolyn says forgiveness is a voluntary process of not seeking revenge. She practices not rehearsing her grudge. She practices seeing her mate, and their relationship, as larger than this traumatic event. She says she practices seeing the good that has come from this disastrous situation—she makes extra efforts to see, and comment on, his positive qualities. On many days she is able to recognize Jack's humanity and vulnerability as well as her own. Although she has a hard time imagining that she could betray him in exactly the same fashion, she understands how she has betrayed him in other ways. She examines her part in their problems. These exercises, she says, draw her closer to him and renew their fragile relationship.

Carolyn has had to be gentle with herself. At first, she required herself to move through the stages of grief one at a time, as if memorizing a lesson from a book. Being a perfectionist and wanting to be a "good Christian," she tried to forgive Jack in record time. This, she thought, would be a testimony to the strength of her faith. She now realizes that pushing herself did not honor her humanity or the magnitude of her wounds.

Carolyn continues to experience a wide range of emotions. But she knows she wants to stay with Jack, learn from this experience, and rebuild their relationship. They are doing well and have great hopes for their future together.

When Only One Is Trying

We cannot talk about healing a hurting relationship without discussing circumstances where only one person seems invested in change. Unfortunately, this frustrating situation is all too common.

Imagine—a woman comes home from work and busies herself preparing the evening meal for her husband and two young children. She is tired from her demanding job as office manager for an expanding dental practice.

She looks at her husband seated in front of the television. She considers starting a conversation, but she knows from experience that he'll just mumble a one-word response. She is preparing to talk to him about counseling, but the last time she did that he laughed at her, saying she was the one with the problem. Alone, she wonders how to repair their fragile and disintegrating relationship. If only they were a team, she thinks, what could their relationship be like?

This scene is common in many households. Two distant people in a damaged relationship—with only one working to repair it. What can someone do in this situation? What steps can you take when you are the one fighting to repair the marriage, but your spouse seems content to let things meander along?

One Person Can Make a Difference

If you notice that you are feeling sorry for yourself, you can roll up your sleeves and get busy changing one thing you *can* change in your relationship—and that is you. You cannot change your mate, but you can change yourself.

Michele Weiner Davis, in her book *The Divorce Remedy*, makes the observation:

> We've been brainwashed to believe that if we talk enough, explain our insights clearly enough, our spouses will finally get it. So, like the Energizer Bunny, we just keep going and going and going. Never mind that what we're doing isn't working or that it's alienating our spouses and making our lives more miserable and lonely. If we're right, we're right, and we're not going to stop proving our points until we've made ourselves perfectly clear.[1]

Thus, camping on being right rather than really working on the relationship, we're focusing on the smoldering match rather than the burning home. Start with you, Davis says. Start with what you can do differently.

How Have You Been Acting?

My suspicion is that, without meaning to, you have actually reinforced his or her negative behavior. Listen to this exchange by a couple I met with recently.

She: "So, are you going to help out around the house tonight or not? I'm getting tired of asking for help."

He: "I was going to clean up the living room. Can you give me a minute?"

She: "Sure. Take all night for all I care."

This scene is ridiculous, you say. It can't really happen like this. Think again. I hear couples talk this way all the time. People become chronically irritated, and their anger and sarcasm spill over into every aspect of their conversation.

Listen to the way you are talking to your mate. How effectively do you share your anger and frustration?

Think Small

Begin by making small changes, such as creating time for "state of the relationship" meetings. Ask questions, share feelings, and encourage your partner to do the same. Find ways to improve the tone of your conversation and the atmosphere in your home. Relationships deteriorate one step at a time, and they are restored the same way.

Consider some of these small tactics for change:

- Talk kindly to your mate at dinner.
- Ask how his or her day went.
- Remember fun things you have done in the past and try them again.
- Offer a gentle touch on the arm or hand with no expectation of more.
- Thank your mate for the opportunity to rebuild the marriage.

Become More Intentional

Harville Hendricks, in his book *Getting the Love You Want,* suggests taking a more observational stance. This includes communicating your needs and desires to your mate, learning to value your mate's needs as highly as you value your own, and searching within yourself for the strengths and abilities you are lacking. He stresses the importance of extricating yourself from the power struggle with your mate. You cannot force your partner to do anything, and in fact, the more you try, the worse the situation will get. He recommends that you begin by owning your own weaknesses rather than focusing on your mate's deficiencies.

You will be amazed by what can happen when you decide to

truly change the way you relate to your mate. By focusing on your own actions, you can make remarkable changes in your partner's behavior. The worst that can happen is that you become much more conscious of the things you are doing that exacerbate the problems in your relationship.

The Art of Transformation

Change and transformation are two very different things. Given the option of simple, cosmetic change and radical, inner and lasting transformation, I opt for the latter. Even though you might be satisfied with change, I want to tease you with the possibility of transformation.

I am reminded of *When the Heart Waits*, the magical book by Sue Monk Kidd. In it, she talked about observing the caterpillar move into the dark night of the soul, that resting place called the chrysalis. She watched the tiny caterpillar, nestled in the crook of a tree branch, spin its coffin. Winter was upon them as the days grew shorter and the nights longer. She spent more days inside; the caterpillar prepared to spend time alone in the darkness of the cocoon. In the stillness, in the damp darkness where apparently nothing was happening, much was changing. A transformation was taking place. Slowly, inexorably, the caterpillar moved from chrysalis to radiant butterfly.

Sometimes transformation takes an entire winter. Sometimes it happens suddenly.

Zacchaeus is mentioned only once in the New Testament, and his story is brief (Luke 19:1-10). He was a small man and an intensely unpopular crook. As a Jewish legman for the Roman IRS, he was someone people went out of their way to avoid. But when Jesus approached, Zacchaeus climbed up a sycamore tree to see Him. When Jesus came to the spot, He looked up, saw Zacchaeus, and told him to come down. "I must stay at your house today." Jesus was agreeing to cavort with a thief? I'm sure the gasps could be heard for miles.

All the people saw this and began to mutter, "He has gone to be the guest of a sinner." And then something incredible happened.

Zacchaeus jumped, or fell, out of the tree. "'Look, Lord. Here and now I give half of my possessions to the poor, and if I have cheated anybody out of anything, I will pay back four times the amount.' Jesus said to him, 'Today salvation has come to this house'" (Luke 19:8-9). What happened to Zacchaeus was not simply change but utter transformation.

What can we take away from the anecdote about the caterpillar or the story of Zacchaeus? The moral is this: Each of us can be transformed inwardly. We can be renewed daily through our faith and belief in Jesus Christ. We don't have to settle for changing from the outside in. We can believe in the transformative process of change from the inside out. Your relationship can experience a similar transformation.

Checkup

Are you willing to do your part to transform your relationship? Although you may be tempted to fuss and fume about your mate, insisting that all would be well if he or she would simply agree to change, you can gain more ground by looking in the mirror.

This chapter has provided powerful tools that can transform your relationship. If you use them properly, they will have an effective impact. Transformation *is* possible. God wants to see your relationship heal and grow, and with His help, it can.

7

I Have a Dream

"I have a dream."

Dr. Martin Luther King spoke these famous words to a crowd amassed on the Washington Mall on a humid day in August 1963. Those words reflected his life. His dream was his passion; his purpose.

His contemporary, President John F. Kennedy, would fall a few months later from an assassin's bullet, leaving a country divided and reeling in pain. People were filled with turmoil, anger, and hatred. The country feared attack from without and division from within.

King sought to unite black and white, rich and poor in a common purpose—to live in equality and peace with one another. This black preacher from Montgomery, Alabama, demonstrated that dreaming could make a difference.

A year before his famous speech in Washington, King was already trying to unify the country.

> We are simply seeking to bring into full realization the American dream—a dream yet unfulfilled. A dream of equality of opportunity, of privilege and property widely

distributed; a dream of a land where men no longer argue that the color of a man's skin determines the content of his character; the dream of a land where every man will respect the dignity and worth of human personality (July 19, 1962).

King challenged the nation to come together, to set aside differences in favor of unification. Today, our call and vision are no less powerful, no less impassioned. Our dream is no less vital. We are working to bring together couples who are divided by huge chasms and insignificant trivialities. With Christ, reconciliation to God and to one another is certainly possible. With God's help, you and your mate can clear a path through the rubble to reconnect with one another.

Having experienced a hurting relationship and learned tools to heal those wounds, you want ways to prevent problems in the future. Upset and saddened by difficulties in your relationship, you are searching for help. Just as Martin Luther King had a dream, I invite you to dream again. To dream of a relationship marked by peace, not dissension. A relationship filled with love and compassion. Believe that with God's help—including the tools you are learning about in this book—you can not only heal current problems but also prevent future breakdowns.

Establish a Vision

Dr. Martin Luther King offered a dream to a fractured nation. He asked us to think larger, to view the future in terms of possibilities. He asked us to look at life as if we were color-blind. I am asking that you set aside ego and selfishness when you look at your relationship. I am asking that you focus instead on the well-being of your mate. Consider the possibility—discord and immaturity give way to peacefulness and thoughtfulness for others, and humility becomes second nature.

Visions and mission statements are important. They offer us a road map for determining if we are on track. This can prevent dissension and brokenness in the future.

My fiancée and I have a vision: *for our speech with one another to be uplifting and encouraging to the other.* Using this as our road map, we have pledged that we will always slow down the process when we start to have an argument. In this way, we can determine whether our language is fitting for building the other up or if it is self-centered and demeaning. For us, being on track means we will monitor how and why we get angry with one another and take care not to use our anger in a hurtful way. We are vigilant about being on track with our vision.

We created a second vision some time ago. We decided *we did not want to tease one another hurtfully.* Having grown up with a brother and three sisters, I learned to tease unmercifully. Having two rough-and-tumble sons only reinforced this style of play. Teasing did not work well in my relationship with Christie, however, having grown up with siblings who teased excessively. So we created a rule not to tease in a way that the other person perceived as hurtful.

Finally, we created a third vision for how we will live once we are married. We decided *to create a home of balance and peacefulness.* We will do this very consciously: by playing certain music, choosing warm colors and fabrics, by not turning on the television, by sharing our love of fine and nutritious foods with good friends, by living on the water. These pieces fit together to form a mosaic—a vision of quiet and thoughtful living.

This is our road map. If I want to prevent tension and turmoil, everything I read, everything I do, must work toward creating our vision.

Conversely, consider how I might feel in these settings:

- A television blares from the family room.
- Raucous music rattles the china.
- A noisy, bustling city is just outside my door.

I don't need to tell you the answer. Obviously, I would not feel at peace. I would not be at my best or be able to bring my best to my relationships.

How about you? What is your vision for your relationship? What qualities will create the perfect backdrop of your relationship?

Not Much Left, but Something

Janelle and Tim came to see me for counseling as a last-ditch effort to save their 24-year marriage.

I sensed little love between them as they sat as far away from each other as possible in my small office. Tim looked tired and drawn. Janelle looked no happier.

"So tell me why you've come to see me," I said.

"We don't want a divorce, but there's not much left between us," Janelle offered.

"When you say, 'There's not much left,' what does that mean?"

Janelle glanced at Tim and continued.

"He does his thing, I do mine. When we do talk, it's about the kids, and they don't even live with us anymore. So you can imagine how quiet things are."

"How long have things been like this?" I asked.

"Too long," Janelle said curtly. "For at least a year."

"This may sound like a dumb question, but how come you do your thing and he does his? Why don't you do 'our' thing?"

This seemed to surprise them. They looked at one another and, for the first time, exchanged smiles.

"Good question," Tim said. "It's just gotten easy for her to go to the office and out to dinner with her girlfriends, and for me to go bowling and golfing with my buddies. When we are together, we don't know what to say. Not good."

"No, not good," I agreed. "Unless you are both happy doing your own thing. I'm assuming you're here because you know a relationship takes work. It takes focus and vision. You have to want to be with one another and do things that feed the relationship."

"Yeah, we haven't been doing that," Tim said.

"You both seem tense, irritated even. Do you feel angry with one another?"

"I can't speak for Tim, but I'm not happy," Janelle said. "I have tried in small ways to create time for us, but it doesn't work, so I go back to my friends. So, yes, I guess I'm upset."

"How about you, Tim?"

"Sure. I don't get the affection I used to get. I don't feel much love, so that makes me mad. Our relationship used to be great, but we let things slide."

"Well, you're here, and you want to save the relationship. If you made it great once, you can make it great again. Are you up for that?"

"We talked the other night about needing to do something about our marriage," Tim said. "We remembered how good things were. We both remember the times when we couldn't wait to be with each other. We used to be best friends. We want that again, so here we are."

"We still care about each other," Janelle said. "We want to build on that and then prevent these problems from occurring again."

"I'm curious," I said. "How did that conversation feel the other night, the one about coming for counseling?"

"It felt good to me," Janelle said. "Tim actually sat down and listened to me for a change."

I saw Tim wince and shrug his shoulders.

"I'm guessing that the way you talk to each other often creates problems. My job will be to help you figure out how to communicate in ways that draw you together. How does that sound?"

"I know I have a sharp tongue," Janelle said. "I get angry and mean. I don't want to be that way."

"We can change that behavior if you're willing," I said.

We spent the next several weeks exploring their history—talking about how they had been a vibrant, happy couple for many years, and what had changed in their relationship. We explored their strengths and weaknesses as a couple. In this chapter we will look at those same qualities—qualities that you can use to repair and prevent problems.

Relationship Management

If relationships were like washing machines, we would buy them new, use and otherwise ignore them for 25 years, and then replace them. Although this kind of thinking has some inherent flaws, it would certainly make relating simpler.

But we all know that relationships are not washing machines. Most of us don't want to hop in and out of relationships even if the pace is once every 25 years. If you have been through a divorce or relationship breakup, you know how grueling it can be. More than likely, you don't want a use-and-replace approach in your relationships.

Relationships require care and upkeep. If you think you can acquire a mate that you admire for a short time and then forget about, you have a lot to learn. Relationships are demanding, but if they are maintained, they will offer plenty of rewards.

In his book *Relationship Rescue*, Dr. Phillip McGraw, known popularly as "Dr. Phil," describes a five-item skill set that you can use to prevent problems and maintain a healthy relationship.

Priority Management

McGraw says that our focus, every day, must be on maintaining a healthy relationship.

> Your rescue of your relationship must be that kind
> of life decision, a priority so important it becomes the
> standard against which you evaluate every thought,

feeling and behavior that you have. You have only to
ask yourself the simple question, "Does this thought,
feeling, or behavior support my priority of maintaining
this relationship?"[1]

What McGraw calls *priority management* I call *focus* or *vision*.
Think about it. If you really, really value something, you take care
of it. For example, you can see what people value by observing how
they spend their time and money. These behaviors invariably provide
telltale signs of what is important in a person's life.

Most of us fail miserably at this test of values. We say we value
our relationship and yet spend precious little time and money on it.
We have been duped into believing we can purchase a relationship,
admire it for a short time, and then allow it to survive on its own.

If you want a healthy relationship—and you are reading this
book because you do—you must change your inner psychology. You
must give up the notion of "use and replace" or "use and ignore."
You must develop a new mentality that thinks like this:

- I want my relationship to be significant and rewarding.
- I am willing to work at this relationship every day to
  make it better.
- I have a high calling to invest in this relationship.
- I will not ignore this relationship but will think about
  ways to make it better and better.

This idea of *priority management* reminds me of my recent decision to lose a few inches around my waist. I had developed Dunlap
disease—my stomach done lapped over my waist—and I didn't like
it. As a psychologist, I routinely counsel men and women on proper
nutrition and weight management. I teach about *the cost of decisions*
such as losing weight. Therefore, I considered my goal and the cost
of making my decision.

I talked to several people before embarking on my journey. I needed to talk things out before making the public vow to lose weight. I had to carefully plan how I would accomplish this task. I travel quite a bit, so maintaining an exercise regimen is challenging. How would I accomplish my goals? Were they so important that I was willing to make a public vow? The answer to the final question was yes, and I mapped out a strategy to attain my objectives. I decided to exercise aerobically at least three days a week and do strength training with weights three additional days—in addition to eating healthily.

Losing weight took the same kind of *priority management* as maintaining a healthy relationship. I decided that fitness was important to me. I created a comprehensive plan and am pleased to say that I am well on my way to achieving my goals.

Behavior Management

This second task for managing your relationship and preventing trouble is called *behavior management*. McGraw encourages people to "act the way you want your life to be." He offers an example: "If you like the way it feels when your partner looks at you and laughs or smiles, then do something that gives your partner the chance to look at you and laugh or smile. Create what you want by doing what you can."[2]

This counsel by Dr. McGraw is not new. Behaviorists have long encouraged depressed people to stop acting depressed. They've told lonely people to stop isolating themselves, anxious people to stop worrying so much, bored people to stop acting disinterested. The analogy works for couples as well: If you want to be a happy couple, be a happy individual.

Simple? Yes! Easy? Not usually. Effective? You bet.

I am currently gulping down heavy doses of books written by SARK, aka Susan Ann Rainbow Kennedy, author of *Wild Succulent Women* and *Eating Mangoes Naked*. What I like so much about SARK's books is her unabashed passion to dive into life headfirst with no life preserver. We live with far too much timidity, she says. Too much waiting for someone else to make us happy. Too much reactivity—"If you upset me, I'll act upset and upset you." She vociferously rejects such behavior.

I recently got into an argument with my fiancée, Christie. Yes, I'm a psychologist and should know better. Don't think I don't tell myself that every time it happens. But it still happens. The start of the fight was, in all likelihood, inconsequential. An overreaction on my part. A sarcastic reaction from her in response. I can't even recall what touched things off. Soon we were caught up in a downward spiral that had us not talking to each other for the better part of an hour.

Finally, we called a halt to our temporary insanity. We looked at each other and said, "This is nuts. Do we really want to keep acting this way?"

She smiled. I smiled back. She reached for my hand. I reached for hers. This was our form of behavior management.

Much of behavior management has to do with reconnecting to one another. Here's what McGraw says:

> The relationship lives or dies in the lifestyle and environment in which it occurs. Creating a new, relationship-friendly lifestyle means making substantial, observable changes... You do not make a difference by wanting different; you make a difference when you do different.[3]

His remarks here are sharp. "You make a difference when you *do* different." Most of us sit back and want something different to come to us. We question why we are not getting the love we want, but in reality we are not *giving* and *doing* the love we want. Take a moment to consider this:

- Are you ready to change the way you behave in your relationship?

- What specific constructive behaviors are you committed to doing?
- Can you measure your behavior changes? If so, how?

Goal Management

Managing your relationship means managing your goals. Specifically, this means having a plan for dealing with the weakest spots in your relationship.

As obvious as this strategy sounds, I find that most couples have no plan for dealing with their weaknesses. They simply amble along, falling into the same potholes on the road time and time again. They relate in a vacuum, unaware and unprepared for the next inevitable struggle. McGraw says that couples must have a "goals plan" that addresses those weaknesses that occur in every relationship.

For example, if you are living in a blended family and tend to fight about how to discipline the kids, you would do well to sit down at a time when emotions are not high and create a plan for handling this aspect of your relationship. Don't wait until tempers flare in the middle of an altercation to create a game plan.

McGraw also recommends having goals that build on the strengths of your relationship. For example, if you believe that your time together on the weekends is one of the most vital parts of your relationship, create goals that have you doing things as a couple on Saturdays and Sundays. If you enjoy your time in church together, make sure you are connected and actively involved in your church.

Thankfully, Christie and I rarely fight. But when we do, the situation can get challenging in a hurry. Our most difficult times invariably occur when we are both tired, overworked, and stressed. Our dash lights flash *warning, warning*. Because we realize this, we are more cautious about taking on an emotional topic when either of us is feeling a bit low. We have agreed to call a time-out if either of us feels defensive. We want to bring our best selves to any conversation, especially one that might include conflict.

We also created our personal "7/13 plan." We agreed to limit any fight to 7 minutes, unless we both agree to extend the time. We also decided that after 13 minutes we would kiss and make up. A silly agreement? Perhaps. Unrealistic? Maybe. But this plan sets clear boundaries by which we relate. I challenge you to create goals that work for your relationship.

Christie and I also find that sharing our faith is very important to us. We have found a church that we both enjoy, and we plan to remain active and involved. We talk frequently about spiritual matters and how they are an integral part of our relationship.

Difference Management

Another important step in relationship management is *difference management*. McGraw offers a unique insight that makes a lot of sense. He says that because men and women are different, no amount of talking or sharing will completely bridge that gap. Sometimes no amount of discussing or cajoling will bring your differing viewpoints into alignment. Even with all of your heartfelt sharing, you still may not understand each other.

The good news is that recognizing this fact will lead to less frustration in your relationship. Quit insisting that your mate always understand you. And quit trying to make your husband or wife always agree with you. It is not going to happen. In fact, the more you try, the more resentment you will create.

Conflict invariably occurs in a relationship when people try to coerce other people into seeing things their way. The more we try to force our point of view, the more distance we create. Feeling coerced and manipulated, our mates will push away.

Divorce often results when one partner says, "We're two different people," or "We have grown apart. We see things so differently." I don't think the differences cause the disasters—the failure to manage them can.

Difference management may be the most powerful prevention tool you can cultivate. I heartily recommend that you sit down with your mate and note your differences. Rather than recoil and moralize about one person being right and the other being wrong, allow each other space to be who you are. Different is okay. It creates a unique flavor in the relationship.

Take a moment to reflect. Consider all the ways you and your mate are different. Note the things your mate does that drive you crazy. Perhaps it is a tendency to be late for engagements. Is that so terrible? Does it really cause that much harm? Perhaps she occasionally overdraws the checking account. Is this really so disastrous? Perhaps he doesn't keep the house quite as clean as you'd like. Is it really that big of a deal?

You get the point. We often complain about our mates, wanting them to be just like us. It isn't going to happen.

Admiration Management

Our final skill for managing your relationship and preventing problems in the future is *admiration management*. Couples in conflict often forget to work at rediscovering and focusing on each other's most admirable qualities. McGraw says, "Couples who deal only with their problems have a problem relationship." This is a profoundly accurate statement.

I know we are often tempted to focus on the negative. Those glaring issues are so… well, glaring! They clamor for our attention, and if we are not extremely vigilant, they will get it. Our weaknesses tend to demand our attention—*all of our attention*. Don't let it happen. Make a priority of creating time and attention for the good things in your relationship. You need "a plan to remind yourself of all your partner's admirable qualities and to remind you that the negative side of your partner doesn't cancel out everything else."[4]

This last point is so very important. When I am angry and intensely disappointed, I cannot see the good qualities of those I care about. I can only see two inches in front of my nose, and the view isn't pleasing. But we can *remind ourselves* of the good things. We can remember to maintain a proper perspective. We don't need to wallow in our myopia. Much better options are available. Focus on your mate's good qualities rather than dwelling on the negatives.

The Scriptures include a variation of this theme. The apostle Paul reminds us, "Whatever is true...whatever is lovely, whatever is admirable—if anything is excellent or praiseworthy—think on such things" (Philippians 4:8). He reminded the church at Galatia about the difference the Spirit could make in their lives: "But the fruit of the Spirit is love, joy, peace, patience, kindness, goodness, faithfulness, gentleness and self-control. Against such things there is no law" (Galatians 5:22).

8
Peering into the Future

Have you had a relationship that over time lost its spark but continued in a "it's probably nothing" frame of mind? Remember, relationships—like cars, washing machines, and computers—will experience their fair share of difficulty. But if you anticipate that trouble and prepare to deal with it, you'll be fine.

Consider your reaction if, when you went in to purchase a car, the salesman told you, "This car will never have any problems. It will run forever and never need any maintenance whatsoever. Your only job will be to keep the gas tank full."

You would either be ecstatic or run for the door in disbelief. The latter would be the preferable option because we all know cars are not trouble free. We know that cars require regular maintenance, and as soon as we forget this truth we are in trouble.

Most of us enter the arena of car ownership knowing we will bump into problems. We may not like the fact, but we're hardly surprised when a tire goes flat, a battery goes dead, or a transmission noise hints at imminent repairs. We don't usually moralize about these problems. We may moan and groan about the costs, but we are hardly surprised to see them come along.

What if we approached relationships with the same mind-set? What if we were candid enough with ourselves to say, "I will approach this relationship with the understanding that it will not be without problems. I agree to face those problems because of the value and benefits my partner brings into my life. I will not be alarmed when trouble comes. I anticipate some issues will arise from the blending of different personalities, and I will greet these problems as opportunities for growth."

You can see the incredible difference such a mind-set would make. A preventative and wholesome attitude of possibility is far superior to an attitude of alarm. Seeing relationships and marriage as opportunities for improvement creates so many more positives than an attitude of dismay and concern.

Are you willing to make that shift in perspective? Will you vow to treat the problems you face today and the ones you will surely face tomorrow as opportunities for God to do some wonderful work in your life?

An oft-quoted portion of the Bible concerning these issues is the first part of the epistle of James. As if reading our minds, James tells us the mind-set we must cultivate:

> Consider it pure joy, my brothers, when you face trials of many kinds, because you know that the testing of your faith develops perseverance. Perseverance must finish its work so that you may be mature and complete, not lacking in anything (James 1:2-4).

Maturity and completeness. This is our reward for enduring and facing the trials that come our way. When we face issues head-on, we grow. When we allow God to use those trials to work on our character, much like a sculptor kneading his clay, we are refined.

Instead of ignoring our problems, we can use them to change for the better.

A Different Road

Many people have heard the story about the man who walked down the road filled with potholes and fell into one. He climbed out, dusted himself off, and vowed not to fall in again.

The next day the man walked down the same road. This time he saw the pothole but stumbled and fell in anyway. He climbed out of the pothole, dusted himself off, and vowed not to fall in the hole again.

The next day, the man walked down the road, spotted the pothole, and tried to walk around it. He tripped over his own feet and fell in. He climbed out of the pothole and vowed to not fall in again.

The next day, the man walked down a different road.

This story makes most of us laugh because it is all too familiar. What is remarkable about the story is that most of us can remember times when we have walked down pothole-filled roads and vowed not to fall in—only to end up smack dab at the bottom of the deepest hole. The curious thing is that most of us construct elaborate schemes to avoid falling into the pothole—trying to walk around it, building a bridge across it, even filling it with concrete. But most of us tenaciously refuse to walk down a different road, thinking naively we can do the same things, expecting different results.

We often have to endure significant pain before we are willing to alter our course. Ben Zander tells the story of Alice Loc Kahana in his book *The Art of Possibility.* An artist now living in Houston, Kahana shared a vivid and painful memory of her horrible journey to Auschwitz when she was 15. On the way, she became separated from her parents and found herself in charge of her eight-year-old brother. When the boxcar arrived, she looked down and noticed he was missing a shoe.

"Why are you so stupid?" she shouted. "Can't you keep track of things?"

Those were the last words that passed between them before they were herded into different cars, never to see one another again.

More than half a century later, Alice Kahana is still living with this horrific memory. She has vowed never again to say anything to a person that could not stand as the last thing she ever said.[1]

The Relationship Doctor's Prescription for Healing a Hurting Relationship is about walking down a different road, saying and doing things differently this time around. It means standing back and realizing that the road you're on has too many potholes and that you'd be better off taking an entirely different route.

Janelle and Tim decided to take a different road. After initiating counseling, they decided to make radical changes in their relationship, remembering their previous joy and working toward recreating it again in the future. In counseling they decided to practice these habits:

- Focus on the good in their marriage—they vowed to catch one another doing positive things in the marriage.

- Not let negative feelings cloud positive ones—they vowed to keep negative concerns in perspective, not letting troublesome molehills become unnecessary mountains.

- Encourage one another—they vowed to find ways to champion one another every day, even if in a small way.

- Develop plans for eliminating negative behaviors—they vowed to tackle the problematic "mountains" one step at a time.

- Develop plans for increasing their relational strengths—they vowed to build on their relational strengths, reminding one another of the special attributes each brought to the relationship.

- Initiate forgiveness and move forward—they vowed not

to bring up past wrongs when emotions ran high. Instead they focused on making the most of the present and future.

- Remember that God is the ultimate author of love—they vowed to maintain the spiritual health of their marriage by church attendance and Bible study together.

These practical steps, practiced one at a time, made a huge difference in their relationship. Their marriage, which was on the brink of divorce, became satisfying to both of them. The core parts of their characters were not substantially different, but the way they treated one another and their focus was radically changed. Janelle and Tim discovered that *a little change goes a long way.*

Inviting Pollyanna to Dinner

We often use the word *Pollyannaish* to negatively refer to someone who is naive and ungrounded. As you may know, the word comes from a character by the same name—Pollyanna—who was a hopeless optimist, someone who believed her glass was always half full. She did not ignore problems; she simply chose to see the brighter side of things. Her view of the world is worth our consideration.

A big part of preventing problems in a relationship, especially those problems that can spiral out of control, has to do with mindset. In fact, one must have the mind-set of possibility—a kind of Pollyannaish attitude that believes anything is possible.

When we see the glass as half full, we are inspired to find solutions to problems. We ask God to help us with what appears to be an impossible task.

But, you say, what if the situation *is* hopeless? What if your mate will simply not change, making the relationship intolerable? I'm not suggesting that you stay in a situation where you are abused, frightened, or mistreated. Being hopeful and creative should never be considered satisfactory remedies for an intolerable reality. Sadly, facing the darkness of reality is sometimes the beginning of positive change.

Short of this, however, being Pollyannaish can be freeing. This freedom—looking expectantly for answers to problems—will be the impetus you need to move forward.

We all know of relationships that endure even though we think they should fail. We are quick to criticize, saying these people should not be together, given how unhappy one or both are. Yet many of these relationships right themselves, and the partners find peace and happiness. They cross over the chasm of anger and escape the tentacles of bitterness and indifference to find a stronger relationship. These are the couples we must talk about. Those who, like Janelle and Tim, have hung in there through the years, sought help, and found victory.

Many proceed with only faint hope. But hope in any measure will help you maintain focus and momentum. With this tenacity, you can move forward to build a solid relationship. And with this experience, you and your mate can prevent problems in the future.

Eyes of Gratefulness

The closing section of this book, reveals perhaps our most powerful strategy for preventing a broken relationship—strengthening your eyes of gratefulness.

As a fairly recent divorcé, I have struggled with singleness. This time has been far different from the singleness I experienced in my early twenties, when life was carefree and dating was an adventure. Although dating in midlife brings a certain amount of excitement, it also brings far more angst. Would I find a soul mate as all the magazine ads touted? If this was so readily available, why had the search been so difficult for me?

Thankfully, I did find my soul mate and can say without hesitation that finding love again is certainly possible. I am grateful to have found Christie. I look around with concern and sadness at many of my single contemporaries who are still looking for their knight in shining armor or princess in waiting. Many have been through countless dates and dating services and have come up short. Love is not as readily available as advertised.

I wonder what would happen if couples were more grateful for what they had. What if they cultivated eyes of gratefulness for one another? Instead of peering over the fence where the grass always appears greener, what if we focused on truly appreciating our mates and our relationships? Robert Wicks, in his book *Everyday Simplicity,* says this:

> There is much we can receive from God if we have "eyes of gratefulness." But if, instead, we face life with a sense of entitlement, we will approach life with demands, expectations and rules regarding what we need to be peaceful and joyful. This sense of entitlement is indeed one of the major enemies of a spiritual attitude. It hardens our souls and keeps us from appreciating the gifts we have been given. A demanding nature can even hurt the very people in our lives who may be offering these gifts to us.[2]

For most of us, our most precious gift, aside from the gift of our Savior, is our mate—yet we fail to recognize it.

"You don't know what you've got 'til it's gone," the saying goes, and we all know that is true. So find ways to sharpen your eyes of gratefulness. Recognize and appreciate what you have in your present partner. Find ways to cultivate the relationship God has given you.

Take a moment and take inventory.

What are the strengths in your relationship? What do you really appreciate about your mate? What would you miss if you were to lose him or her? Thank God for the gift of your mate. He or she can never be replaced.

The apostle Paul says it clearly: "I pray also that the eyes of your heart may be enlightened in order that you may know the hope to which he has called you, the riches of his glorious inheritance in the saints, and his incomparably great power of us who believe" (Ephesians 1:18-19).

I pray this same prayer for you now. I pray that you may know the hope that we have as believers in Jesus Christ—He promises never to leave you or forsake you. I pray that you will know His comforting presence in your life.

Checkup

I hope you have enjoyed our time together. You are now equipped with skills you can use to change your relationship. You can reverse all of the mistakes you and your mate have made, all of the troublesome patterns you have repeated again and again. It is never too late to have a wonderful relationship.

Start today. Start small. Start with an achievable plan that you practice day in and day out. Start with prayer and the blessings of God. But start.

May God bless you in your journey of healing.

Notes

Chapter 1—The Four Horsemen of a Relational Apocalypse

1. John Gottman, *Why Marriages Succeed or Fail* (New York: Simon & Schuster, 1994), 74.
2. Ibid., 79.
3. Ibid., 94.

Chapter 2—Men, Women, and Stress

1. John Gray, *Men, Women and Relationships* (Portland, OR: Beyond Words Publishing, 1993), 128.
2. Ibid., 133.
3. Ibid., 136.
4. Ibid., 140.

Chapter 3—Where Did We Go Wrong?

1. David Viscott, *I Love You, Let's Work It Out* (New York: Simon and Schuster, 1987), 172.

Chapter 4—When Trying to Help Just Makes Things Worse

1. Scott Peck, *The Road Less Traveled* (New York: Simon and Schuster, 1978), 84.

Chapter 6—The Art of Communication

1. Michele Weiner Davis, *The Divorce Remedy* (New York: Simon & Schuster, 2001), 70.

Chapter 7—I Have a Dream

1. Phillip McGraw, *Relationship Rescue* (New York: Hyperion, 2000), 252.
2. Ibid., 255.
3. Ibid., 256.
4. Ibid., 264.

Chapter 8—Peering into the Future

1. Ben Zander, *The Art of Possibility* (New York: Penguin Books, 2000), 174.

2. Robert Wicks, *Everyday Simplicity* (Notre Dame: Sorin Books, 2000), 52.

Dr. Hawkins is interested in
hearing about your journey and may be
contacted through his website at
www.YourRelationshipDoctor.com